Table of Contents

III

"And whatsoever we ask, we receive of him, because we keep his commandments, and do those things that are pleasing in his sight, KJV 1 John 3:22."

Table of Contents

IV

"And whatsoever we ask, we receive of him, because we keep his commandments, and do those things that are pleasing in his sight, KJV 1 John 3:22."

Beware of the Pink Assassin (Your Tongue): The True Vine (Yashu'a, Jesus) Power of Life and Death is in the Tongue; Speaking God's (אלהים Eloّhîym) "Will" for Your Life into Existence!

CHILDREN OF THE MOST HIGH:
PRISTINE YOUTH AND FAMILY SOLUTIONS, LLC.
SONS AND DAUGHTERS OF THE MOST HIGH PUBLISHERS ®

Oh, Gracious Most High Heavenly father, Holy is your name, Your Will Be Done Now and Forever!

By

Woodie Hughes Jr.
CEO & Founder of the Children of the Most High:
Pristine Youth and Family Solutions LLC.
Sons and Daughters of the Most High Publishers®
Mr. Hughes is a Servant of the Most High, and a Teacher of the Most High's Doctrine.

I

"And whatsoever we ask, we receive of him, because we keep his commandments, and do those things that are pleasing in his sight, KJV 1 John 3:22."

Beware of the Pink Assassin (Your Tongue): The True Vine
(Yashu'a, Jesus) Power of Life and Death is in the Tongue;
Speaking God's (אלהים Elóhîym) "Will"
for Your Life into Existence!

Editor: Sons and Daughters of the Most High Editors

ISBN: 978-1-948355-04-9
Library of Congress Control Number: 2020916258

FOR MORE INFORMATION CONTACT:

Woodie Hughes Jr., CEO & Founder of the Children of the
Most High: Pristine Youth and Family Solutions, LLC.
Sons and Daughters of the Most High Publishers ®

Online ordering is available for all products at our Amazon
Store Front on our website at: childrenofthemosthigh.com
Or, write to us at: Children of the Most High: Pristine Youth
and Family Solutions, LLC. P.O. Box 6365, Warner Robins,
Georgia 31095.

II
**"And whatsoever we ask, we receive of him,
because we keep his commandments, and do those
things that are pleasing in his sight, KJV 1 John 3:22."**

Table of Contents

V
"And whatsoever we ask, we receive of him, because we keep his commandments, and do those things that are pleasing in his sight, KJV 1 John 3:22."

Beware of the Pink Assassin: The True Vine (Yashu'a, Jesus)
Power of Life and Death is in the Tongue;
**Speaking God's (אלהים Elôhîym) "Will"
for Your Life into Existence!**

CHILDREN OF THE MOST HIGH:
PRISTINE YOUTH AND FAMILY SOLUTIONS, LLC.
SONS AND DAUGHTERS OF THE MOST HIGH PUBLISHERS ®

*Oh, Gracious Most High Heavenly father, Holy is your name,
Your Will Be Done Now and Forever!*

Greetings:

We greet all members of humanity in peace! Nothing would exist if you Oh Gracious Most High Heavenly Father, The Creator didn't create it. You are alone in Your Greatness; you have no partners that share in your grace. To you all sovereignty is due and you are all powerful over everything. We seek refuge in you, the ever watchful Most High who hears and knows all things! Glory be to you as many times as the number of things you have created! All gratitude is due to you oh gracious Most High Heavenly Father, you are the Creator and Sustainer of all the boundless universes. You are the Yielder, and the most Merciful. The Ruler of the Day of Judgement. It's you whom we worship and it is you alone whom we beseech for help. Oh Guide, guide us to the narrow path **which reflects moral integrity and positive character traits in action** of the ones who stand straight, the narrow path of those who earned your grace not inclusive of those who brought an everlasting curse on themselves, those who conceal the facts of that which they know to be true in order to lead the **sincere-hearted seekers** of your truth astray. Amen

1

**"And whatsoever we ask, we receive of him,
because we keep his commandments, and do those
things that are pleasing in his sight, KJV 1 John 3:22."**

Beware of the Pink Assassin (Your Tongue): The True Vine
(Yashu'a, Jesus) Power of Life and Death is in the Tongue;
Speaking God's (אלהים Elohîym) "Will"
for Your Life into Existence!

CHILDREN OF THE MOST HIGH:
PRISTINE YOUTH AND FAMILY SOLUTIONS, LLC.
SONS AND DAUGHTERS OF THE MOST HIGH PUBLISHERS ®

Oh, Gracious Most High Heavenly father, Holy is your name,
Your Will Be Done Now and Forever!

**What does the phrase: "those who earned your grace" mean
as oppose to saying "those who receive your grace?"** The
word: "**grace**" in the King James Version (KJV) bible book of
Genesis chapter 6 verse 8 is: חֵן **Khane** or **chen** pronounced as
khān (KJV bible Hebrew Strong's Concordance#2580). The
word: "חֵן **Khane** or **chen**" means "**favor, kindness.**" The
word: "grace" in the KJV bible book of John chapter 1 verse
17 is: χάρις **Kharece** or **charis** pronounced as **khä'-rēs (KJV
bible Greek Strong's Concordance#5485).** The word: "χάρις
Kharece or **charis**" means "**joy, delight.**" So, the phrase:
"those who earned your grace" is in reference **to those people
who are no longer physically alive that have transitioned to
a higher life such as: Yashu'a (Jesus), John the Baptist,
Yowkhanan Bar Zebedee (John Son of Zebedee who was
Yashu'a (Jesus) beloved disciple), or Ab-Ra-Kham
(Abraham).** The phrase: "**those who receive your grace**" is in
reference **to any person or people** who the Most High
Heavenly Father bestows **favor** on by allowing them to still be
physically alive, and to have an opportunity to experience **joy**
while still be physically alive.

2

**"And whatsoever we ask, we receive of him,
because we keep his commandments, and do those
things that are pleasing in his sight, KJV 1 John 3:22."**

Beware of the Pink Assassin (Your Tongue): The True Vine (Yashu'a, Jesus) Power of Life and Death is in the Tongue;

Speaking God's (אלהים Elôhîym) "Will" for Your Life into Existence!

CHILDREN OF THE MOST HIGH:
PRISTINE YOUTH AND FAMILY SOLUTIONS, LLC.
SONS AND DAUGHTERS OF THE MOST HIGH PUBLISHERS ❧

Oh, Gracious Most High Heavenly father, Holy is your name,
Your Will Be Done Now and Forever!

Dedication

The "**Beware of the Pink Assassin (The Tongue): The Power of Life and Death is in the Tongue; Speaking God's (אלהים Elôhîym) "Will" for Your Life into Existence!**" book is dedicated to all youth and all adults who are children of the Most High that want to learn the doctrine of the **Most High (ELYOWN עֶלְיוֹן) God (EL אֵל)** in a way that reflects the original languages of the bible before being translated into the English language, and that reflects the original Most High Heavenly Father's doctrine that **Yashu'a Ha Mashiakh (Jesus the Messiah)** taught. In the KJV bible book of Genesis chapter 14 verse 18 states: "And Melchizedek king of Salem brought forth bread and wine: and he *was* the priest of the **Most High** God."

3

"And whatsoever we ask, we receive of him, because we keep his commandments, and do those things that are pleasing in his sight, KJV 1 John 3:22."

CHILDREN OF THE MOST HIGH:
PRISTINE YOUTH AND FAMILY SOLUTIONS, LLC.
SONS AND DAUGHTERS OF THE MOST HIGH PUBLISHERS ®

Oh, Gracious Most High Heavenly father, Holy is your name, Your Will Be Done Now and Forever!

The title: "**Most High**" is: the KJV bible Hebrew Strong's Concordance#**5945** for the title: "**Most High**" (**ELYOWN** עֶלְיוֹן **EL** אֵל), which means: "Highest, Most High, <u>Name of God</u>, as title, <u>The Supreme</u>: — (Most, on) high (-er, -est), upper(-most)." The title: "**God'** <u>in this verse</u> is the KJV bible Hebrew Strong's Concordance#**5945** for the title: "**God**" (**EL** אֵל), which means: "God, god, power, mighty, goodly, great, idols, might, strong, god, god-like one, mighty one, mighty men, men of rank, mighty heroes, angels, god, false god, (demons, imaginations), and mighty things in nature."

4

"And whatsoever we ask, we receive of him, because we keep his commandments, and do those things that are pleasing in his sight, KJV 1 John 3:22."

Beware of the Pink Assassin (Your Tongue): The True Vine
(Yashu'a, Jesus) Power of Life and Death is in the Tongue;
Speaking God's (אלהים Elóhîym) "Will"
for Your Life into Existence!

CHILDREN OF THE MOST HIGH:
PRISTINE YOUTH AND FAMILY SOLUTIONS, LLC.
SONS AND DAUGHTERS OF THE MOST HIGH PUBLISHERS ®

Oh, Gracious Most High Heavenly father, Holy is your name,
Your Will Be Done Now and Forever!

Acknowledgements

We thank the Most High Heavenly Father who is: **The Most
High Heavenly One, the Sustainer, the Nourisher, the
Provider of Life**, and **the Creator of the boundless universes**,
thank you for sending the Messiah Yashu'a (Jesus) who was a
willing sacrifice, and for your angelic-beings that protect us,
inspire us and guide us to obey you, inclusive of the **Sun of
Righteousness** (the word for "**Sun**" is **Shemesh** צְדָקָה
pronounced **Sheh'·mesh**, the word for "**Righteousness**" is
Tsĕdaqah שֶׁמֶשׁ pronounced **Tsed·ä·kä'**) who arises with
healing in his wings as stated in the King James Version (KJV)
bible book of **Malachi chapter 4 verse 2**, and we thank the
Most High Heavenly One for life, for health and for everything
else!

5

**"And whatsoever we ask, we receive of him,
because we keep his commandments, and do those
things that are pleasing in his sight, KJV 1 John 3:22."**

Beware of the Pink Assassin (Your Tongue): The True Vine
(Yashu'a, Jesus) Power of Life and Death is in the Tongue;
Speaking God's (אלהים Elốhîym) "Will"
for Your Life into Existence!

CHILDREN OF THE MOST HIGH:
PRISTINE YOUTH AND FAMILY SOLUTIONS, LLC.
SONS AND DAUGHTERS OF THE MOST HIGH PUBLISHERS ®

Oh, Gracious Most High Heavenly father, Holy is your name,
Your Will Be Done Now and Forever!

A Special Thank You to: My Dad (**The Honorable**: **Mr.**
Woodie Hughes Sr.), and Mom (**The Noble**: **Mrs. Annette**
Hughes) for accepting the Messiah Yashu'a (Jesus) and raising
me and my brothers in a Godly home filled with love as they
like the Messiah Yashu'a (Jesus); willingly sacrificed their
youth and many worldly possessions to ensure that my brothers
and I had the greatest opportunity to achieve the maximum
levels of success in all areas of our lives; **thank you Mom and**
Dad!

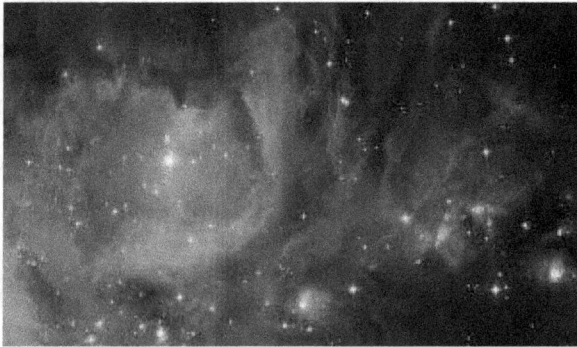

6
"And whatsoever we ask, we receive of him,
because we keep his commandments, and do those
things that are pleasing in his sight, KJV 1 John 3:22."

Beware of the Pink Assassin (Your Tongue): The True Vine (Yashu'a, Jesus) Power of Life and Death is in the Tongue; Speaking God's (אלהים Elóhîym) "Will" for Your Life into Existence!

CHILDREN OF THE MOST HIGH:
PRISTINE YOUTH AND FAMILY SOLUTIONS, LLC.
SONS AND DAUGHTERS OF THE MOST HIGH PUBLISHERS ®

Oh, Gracious Most High Heavenly father, Holy is your name,
Your Will Be Done Now and Forever!

A Special Thank You to: **My Beloved Wife and best friend (Mrs. Tonya L. Hughes)** who sacrificed her health and well-being to give birth to our children. Our children inspire me every day to keep working hard for our family and to continuously work hard to help uplift members of humanity so that we can work together to help people and the planet earth to maintain, and sustain positive health and balance for that great day, when: "Thy kingdom will come to earth as it is in heaven." We also thank the many other family members, friends, colleagues, mentors, and global spiritual family who are the children of the Most High and who are in the body of Christ.

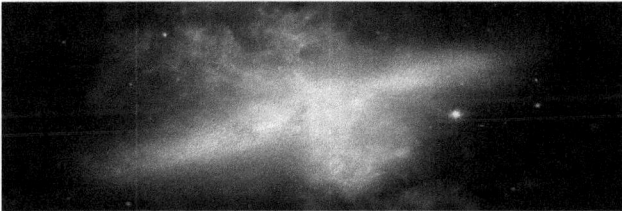

7

"And whatsoever we ask, we receive of him, because we keep his commandments, and do those things that are pleasing in his sight, KJV 1 John 3:22."

Beware of the Pink Assassin (Your Tongue): The True Vine (Yashu'a, Jesus) Power of Life and Death is in the Tongue; Speaking God's (אלהים Elóhîym) "Will" for Your Life into Existence!

CHILDREN OF THE MOST HIGH:
PRISTINE YOUTH AND FAMILY SOLUTIONS, LLC.
SONS AND DAUGHTERS OF THE MOST HIGH PUBLISHERS ®

Oh, Gracious Most High Heavenly father, Holy is your name, Your Will Be Done Now and Forever!

Who are the Children of the Most High Pristine Youth and Family Solutions, LLC.?

We are teachers of the doctrine of the Most High; the doctrine that the real Messiah Yashu'a (Jesus) taught. In the KJV bible book of John chapter 7 verse 16; the Messiah Yashu'a (Jesus) stated: "My doctrine isn't mine, but his that sent me." The Children of the Most High, Pristine Youth and Family Solutions, LLC. purpose is to do the Most High Heavenly Father's will only! We exist and work under the authority of the Most High Heavenly Father, who is the Creator and the Ruler of all of the boundless universes! We acknowledge the Messiah Jesus as our Savior who **we refer to** in his original Judean/Galilean Aramaic (Hebrew) language birth name **Yasu'a** or **Yashu'a** (ישוע) meaning "**Savior**" and **Jesus,** who is **the Son of God** in English.

8

"And whatsoever we ask, we receive of him, because we keep his commandments, and do those things that are pleasing in his sight, KJV 1 John 3:22."

Beware of the Pink Assassin (Your Tongue): The True Vine (Yashu'a, Jesus) Power of Life and Death is in the Tongue; Speaking God's (אלהים Elòhîym) "Will" for Your Life into Existence!

CHILDREN OF THE MOST HIGH:
PRISTINE YOUTH AND FAMILY SOLUTIONS, LLC.
SONS AND DAUGHTERS OF THE MOST HIGH PUBLISHERS ®

Oh, Gracious Most High Heavenly father, Holy is your name, Your Will Be Done Now and Forever!

We have accepted the Lord Jesus Christ (Yashu'a Ha Mashiakh – Jesus the Messiah or Yehoshu'a, which means Yahayyu is Salvation or Yahayyu Saves) as our Savior and we are in the Body of Christ!

CHILDREN OF THE MOST HIGH:
PRISTINE YOUTH AND FAMILY SOLUTIONS, LLC.
SONS AND DAUGHTERS OF THE MOST HIGH PUBLISHERS ®

What is the Mission, Vision, and Motto of the Children of the Most High; Pristine Youth and Family Solutions, LLC?

The Mission is: To inspire and empower all children of the Most High to pristinely make the world a safe and healthy place for all members of humanity.

9

"And whatsoever we ask, we receive of him, because we keep his commandments, and do those things that are pleasing in his sight, KJV 1 John 3:22."

Beware of the Pink Assassin (Your Tongue): The True Vine
(Yashu'a, Jesus) Power of Life and Death is in the Tongue;
Speaking God's (אלהים Elóhîym) "Will"
for Your Life into Existence!

CHILDREN OF THE MOST HIGH:
PRISTINE YOUTH AND FAMILY SOLUTIONS, LLC.
SONS AND DAUGHTERS OF THE MOST HIGH PUBLISHERS ®

Oh, Gracious Most High Heavenly father, Holy is your name,
Your Will Be Done Now and Forever!

The Vision is: To create a world that is ruled by Love and the
"Will" of the Most High, void of negative emotions, greed, lusts
and love of money. According to the KJV bible book of
Matthew chapter 19 verse 26, the Messiah Yashu'a (Jesus) said
unto them, "With men this is impossible; but with God all
things are possible." According to the KJV bible book of
Philippians chapter 4 verse 13; it states: "I can do all things
through Christ which strengthened me." Therefore; with God
and through Christ, the children of the Most High Pristine
Youth and Family Solutions, LLC. Mission and Vision can
become a reality for the children of the Most High!

Motto: There is no right way to do the wrong thing!

10
**"And whatsoever we ask, we receive of him,
because we keep his commandments, and do those
things that are pleasing in his sight, KJV 1 John 3:22."**

Beware of the Pink Assassin (Your Tongue): The True Vine (Yashu'a, Jesus) Power of Life and Death is in the Tongue;
Speaking God's (אלהים Elóhîym) "Will"
for Your Life into Existence!

CHILDREN OF THE MOST HIGH:
PRISTINE YOUTH AND FAMILY SOLUTIONS, LLC.
SONS AND DAUGHTERS OF THE MOST HIGH PUBLISHERS ®

Oh, Gracious Most High Heavenly father, Holy is your name,
Your Will Be Done Now and Forever!

Who is the Most High to the Children of the Most High Pristine Youth and Family Solutions, LLC.?

The Most High Heavenly Father is Love, the Sustainer, the Nourisher, the Provider of all Life, and the Omnipotent and the Omnipresent Creator of the boundless universes. The Most High Heavenly Father encompasses and interpenetrates all existence inclusive of every part of nature both visible as well as invisible. Oh, Most High Heavenly Father, you are all, and there is nothing nearer to us than you; for you encompass all things! Glory be to you alone! In the KJV bible book of John chapter 4 verse 23, the Messiah Yashu'a (Jesus) said: "God is a Spirit: and they that worship him must worship him in spirit and in truth."

11

"And whatsoever we ask, we receive of him,
because we keep his commandments, and do those
things that are pleasing in his sight, KJV 1 John 3:22."

Beware of the Pink Assassin (Your Tongue): The True Vine (Yashu'a, Jesus) Power of Life and Death is in the Tongue;

Speaking God's (אלהים Elohîym) "Will" for Your Life into Existence!

CHILDREN OF THE MOST HIGH:
PRISTINE YOUTH AND FAMILY SOLUTIONS, LLC.
SONS AND DAUGHTERS OF THE MOST HIGH PUBLISHERS ®

Oh, Gracious Most High Heavenly father, Holy is your name,
Your Will Be Done Now and Forever!

In the KJV bible book of Genesis, chapter 14 verse 18 states: "And Melchizedek (**Malkiy-Tsedeq**, מַלְכִּי־צֶדֶק) king of Salem brought forth bread and wine: and he was the priest of the **Most High** (**ELYOWN** עֶלְיוֹן) **God** (**EL** אֵל)."

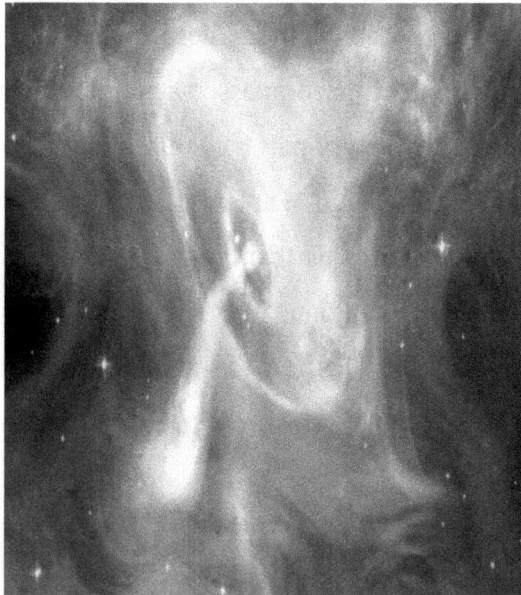

12

"And whatsoever we ask, we receive of him, because we keep his commandments, and do those things that are pleasing in his sight, KJV 1 John 3:22."

Beware of the Pink Assassin (Your Tongue): The True Vine (Yashu'a, Jesus) Power of Life and Death is in the Tongue; Speaking God's (אלהים Elohȋym) "Will" for Your Life into Existence!

CHILDREN OF THE MOST HIGH:
PRISTINE YOUTH AND FAMILY SOLUTIONS, LLC.
SONS AND DAUGHTERS OF THE MOST HIGH PUBLISHERS ®

Oh, Gracious Most High Heavenly father, Holy is your name, Your Will Be Done Now and Forever!

Who is the Real Messiah Jesus to the Children of the Most High Pristine Youth and Family Solutions, LLC.?

The Children of the Most High, Pristine Youth and Family Solutions, LLC., acknowledges the Real Messiah Jesus as our Savior who **we refer to** in his original Galilean/Judean Aramic (Hebrew) language, original birth name **Yasu'a (يسوع)** or **Yashu'a (יְשׁוּעַ)** meaning "**Savior**" also spelled Yeshua or Yehoshu'a, **Iesous** ('Ιησοῦς) in the Greek translation and as **Kurios** (Greek word for Lord), and **Issa** or **Isa** in Ashuric Syriac (Arabic). Now when **Yehoshu'a** is translated in the Hebrew language it translates as **Yahayyu Saves** or simply **Joshua**, and in the Galilean language as Yashu'a or **Yasu'a** Inar **Rab** (which translates as **Jesus Son of the Sustainer**), Yashu'a Bar Yahayyu (با حـــ, Existing One).

13
"And whatsoever we ask, we receive of him, because we keep his commandments, and do those things that are pleasing in his sight, KJV 1 John 3:22."

Beware of the Pink Assassin (Your Tongue): The True Vine
(Yashu'a, Jesus) Power of Life and Death is in the Tongue;
Speaking God's (אלהים Elóhîym) "Will"
for Your Life into Existence!

CHILDREN OF THE MOST HIGH:
PRISTINE YOUTH AND FAMILY SOLUTIONS, LLC.
SONS AND DAUGHTERS OF THE MOST HIGH PUBLISHERS ®

Oh, Gracious Most High Heavenly father, Holy is your name,
Your Will Be Done Now and Forever!

In Modern Hebrew translates as **Savior Son of the Everliving**
or **Savior Son of the Existing One** or **Living One**, **Yasu'** and
Haru as **Karast "Christ"** to the **Ancient** original indigenous
Egyptian people of what is called: "Egypt" today, not to be
confused with the Egyptians who are the nonindigenous people
who migrated to what is now known as Egypt. Yashu'a called
Jesus, is **the Son of God** in English. Yashu'a (Jesus), **the Son**
of the Most High God is the way back to the Most High. In the
KJV bible book of John chapter 14 verse 6; the Messiah
Yashu'a (Jesus) said: "I am the way, the truth, and the life:
no man (the words: "no man" is not in the original language
that this verse was revealed in. The original word for "no man"
in the Greek KJV bible translation is: "**Oudeis**" (οὐδείς, Oudeis
(is the KJV bible Greek Strong's Concordance#**3762**) means:
not one; no one, nothing.

14

"And whatsoever we ask, we receive of him,
because we keep his commandments, and do those
things that are pleasing in his sight, KJV 1 John 3:22."

Beware of the Pink Assassin (Your Tongue): The True Vine (Yashu'a, Jesus) Power of Life and Death is in the Tongue; Speaking God's (אלהים Elóhîym) "Will" for Your Life into Existence!

CHILDREN OF THE MOST HIGH:
PRISTINE YOUTH AND FAMILY SOLUTIONS, LLC.
SONS AND DAUGHTERS OF THE MOST HIGH PUBLISHERS ®

Oh, Gracious Most High Heavenly father, Holy is your name, Your Will Be Done Now and Forever!

So, this phrase is inclusive of males and females, not just males) cometh unto the Father, but by me." However, according to the Messiah Yashu'a (Jesus), no one can come to him unless the Most High Heavenly Father sends them to him. Yashu'a (Jesus) said in the KJV bible book of John chapter 6 verse 44: "No man (οὐδείς **oudeis**) can (δύναμαι *dynamai*) come (ἔρχομαι *erchomai*) to (πρός *pros*) me (μέ **mé, meh**), except (ἐὰν μή *ean mē*);" "KJV bible Greek Strong's Concordance#**3362** meaning: **if not, unless, whoever... not**) the Father which hath sent me draw (ἕλκω *helkō*; KJV bible Greek Strong's Concordance#**1670** meaning: **to draw by inward power, lead, impel; to drag (literally or figuratively)** him: and I will raise him up at the last day." Again, in the aforementioned verse, the words: "no man" is not in the original language that this verse was revealed in.

15

"And whatsoever we ask, we receive of him, because we keep his commandments, and do those things that are pleasing in his sight, KJV 1 John 3:22."

Beware of the Pink Assassin (Your Tongue): The True Vine (Yashu'a, Jesus) Power of Life and Death is in the Tongue; **Speaking God's (אלהים Elôhîym) "Will" for Your Life into Existence!**

CHILDREN OF THE MOST HIGH:
PRISTINE YOUTH AND FAMILY SOLUTIONS, LLC.
SONS AND DAUGHTERS OF THE MOST HIGH PUBLISHERS ®

Oh, Gracious Most High Heavenly father, Holy is your name, Your Will Be Done Now and Forever!

The original word for "no man" is: "**Oudeis**" (οὐδείς, Oudeis (KJV bible Greek Strong's Concordance#**3762**) means: *not one*; *no one, nothing*.

What does the Children of the Most High Pristine Youth and Family Solutions, LLC. do?

The Children of the Most High; Pristine Youth and Family Solutions LLC. does the will of the Most High Heavenly Father. We are **Teachers** and **Administrators** of the Most High Doctrine and work diligently to teach youth and adults how to solve problems, and how to successfully work through difficult problems or issues or situations by utilizing the **Children of the Most High Pristine Youth and Family Solutions, LLC. 9X9 True Vine "Yashu'a" (Jesus) B.A. (Soul) K.A. (Spirit) R.E. (Sun) ("RE" is pronounced as "RAY") Sequential Order of Learning.**

16

"And whatsoever we ask, we receive of him, because we keep his commandments, and do those things that are pleasing in his sight, KJV 1 John 3:22."

Beware of the Pink Assassin (Your Tongue): The True Vine
(Yashu'a, Jesus) Power of Life and Death is in the Tongue;
Speaking God's (אלהים Elóhîym) "Will"
for Your Life into Existence!

CHILDREN OF THE MOST HIGH:
PRISTINE YOUTH AND FAMILY SOLUTIONS, LLC.
SONS AND DAUGHTERS OF THE MOST HIGH PUBLISHERS ®

*Oh, Gracious Most High Heavenly father, Holy is your name,
Your Will Be Done Now and Forever!*

**More information about the True Vine "Yashu'a" (Jesus)
B.A.-K.A.-R.E. Sequential Order of Learning will be
expounded on in chapter 9.** Our targeted audiences are youth
(who are between the 5th and 12th grades) and adults who are
children of the Most High. So, we teach in an effort to make the
doctrine of the Most High clear in the minds of people who want
to learn the original message or messages of the scriptures before
they were translated into other languages, and we teach in an
effort to create an opportunity for them to learn how to apply the
doctrine of the Most High in all that they aspire to do!

17

**"And whatsoever we ask, we receive of him,
because we keep his commandments, and do those
things that are pleasing in his sight, KJV 1 John 3:22."**

Beware of the Pink Assassin (Your Tongue): The True Vine
(Yashu'a, Jesus) Power of Life and Death is in the Tongue;
Speaking God's (אלהים Elohíym) "Will"
for Your Life into Existence!

CHILDREN OF THE MOST HIGH:
PRISTINE YOUTH AND FAMILY SOLUTIONS, LLC.
SONS AND DAUGHTERS OF THE MOST HIGH PUBLISHERS ®

Oh, Gracious Most High Heavenly father, Holy is your name,
Your Will Be Done Now and Forever!

Why does the Children of the Most High Pristine Youth and Family Solutions, LLC. refer to themselves as <u>T</u>eachers / <u>A</u>dministers of the Most High Heavenly Father's Doctrine instead of <u>P</u>reachers?

The Children of the Most High Pristine Youth and Family Solutions, LLC. refer to themselves as <u>T</u>eachers and **<u>A</u>dministers of the Most High Heavenly Father's Doctrine** that Yashu'a (Jesus) taught instead of <u>P</u>reachers because the Most High inspired and endowed them with the knowledge and with the ability to teach with the True-Vine (Yashu'a, Jesus) Spirit of the Word of Knowledge in the KJV bible book of 1st Corinthians chapter 12 verse 8 to teach the Most High's Doctrine as mentioned in the KJV bible book of John chapter 7 verse 16.

18

"And whatsoever we ask, we receive of him, because we keep his commandments, and do those things that are pleasing in his sight, KJV 1 John 3:22."

Beware of the Pink Assassin (Your Tongue): The True Vine (Yashu'a, Jesus) Power of Life and Death is in the Tongue; Speaking God's (אלהים Elổhîym) "Will" for Your Life into Existence!

CHILDREN OF THE MOST HIGH:
PRISTINE YOUTH AND FAMILY SOLUTIONS, LLC.
SONS AND DAUGHTERS OF THE MOST HIGH PUBLISHERS ®

Oh, Gracious Most High Heavenly father, Holy is your name, Your Will Be Done Now and Forever!

In the KJV bible book of Matthews chapter 28 verses 19-20, the Messiah Yashu'a (Jesus) said: "Go ye therefore, and teach all nations, baptizing them in the name of the Father, and of the Son, and of the Holy Ghost. Teaching them to observe all things whatsoever I have commanded you: and, lo, I am with you always, even unto the end of the world. Amen." The word in the aforementioned KJV bible book of Matthews chapter 28 verse 19 for *teach* is: the **KJV bible Greek Strong's Concordance#3100 mathēteuō (μαθητεύω) which means: teach, instruct, be disciple**.

19

"And whatsoever we ask, we receive of him, because we keep his commandments, and do those things that are pleasing in his sight, KJV 1 John 3:22."

Beware of the Pink Assassin (Your Tongue): The True Vine
(Yashu'a, Jesus) Power of Life and Death is in the Tongue;
Speaking God's (אלהים Elŏhîym) "Will"
for Your Life into Existence!

*Oh, Gracious Most High Heavenly father, Holy is your name,
Your Will Be Done Now and Forever!*

The word in the book of Matthews chapter 28 verse 20 for
Teaching is: the **KJV bible Greek Strong's
Concordance#1321 didaskō (διδάσκω) which means: to
teach, to hold discourse with others in order to instruct
them, deliver didactic discourses, to be a teacher, to
discharge the office of a teacher, conduct one's self as a
teacher, to teach one, to impart instruction, instill doctrine
into one, the thing taught or enjoined, to explain or expound
a thing, to teach one something.**

20

"And whatsoever we ask, we receive of him,
because we keep his commandments, and do those
things that are pleasing in his sight, KJV 1 John 3:22."

Beware of the Pink Assassin (Your Tongue): The True Vine (Yashu'a, Jesus) Power of Life and Death is in the Tongue; Speaking God's (אלהים Eloʾhiym) "Will" for Your Life into Existence!

CHILDREN OF THE MOST HIGH:
PRISTINE YOUTH AND FAMILY SOLUTIONS, LLC.
SONS AND DAUGHTERS OF THE MOST HIGH PUBLISHERS

Oh, Gracious Most High Heavenly father, Holy is your name, Your Will Be Done Now and Forever!

The word for **"Preach"** in the KJV bible book of Matthew chapter 11 verse 1 is: the **KJV bible Greek Strong's Concordance#2784 kērysso (κηρύσσω) which means to: preach, publish, and proclaim.** In the KJV bible book of Matthew chapter 11 verse 1; it states: "And it came to pass, when Jesus had made an end of commanding his twelve disciples, he departed thence to **teach** and to **preach** in their cities. The plural noun of **"teach"** is **"Teachers"**: the **KJV bible Greek Strong's Concordance#1320 didaskalos** (διδάσκαλος, meaning one who teaches or teachers) and has the same root foundation as the word for "Teach" (the **KJV bible Greek Strong's Concordance#1321 didaskō** **(διδάσκω)** in the book of Acts chapter 13 verse 1; and states:

21
"And whatsoever we ask, we receive of him, because we keep his commandments, and do those things that are pleasing in his sight, KJV 1 John 3:22."

Beware of the Pink Assassin (Your Tongue): The True Vine (Yashu'a, Jesus) Power of Life and Death is in the Tongue; **Speaking God's (אלהים Elŏhîym) "Will" for Your Life into Existence!**

CHILDREN OF THE MOST HIGH:
PRISTINE YOUTH AND FAMILY SOLUTIONS, LLC.
SONS AND DAUGHTERS OF THE MOST HIGH PUBLISHERS ®

Oh, Gracious Most High Heavenly father, Holy is your name, Your Will Be Done Now and Forever!

"Now there were in the church that was at Antioch certain prophets and **teachers**; as Barnabas, and Simeon that was called **Niger**, and Lucius of Cyrene, and Manaen, which had been brought up with Herod the tetrarch, and Saul." In the aforementioned verse, the word: "**Niger**" is the **KJV Bible Greek Strong's Concordance#3526 Νίγερ (Niger)** which means: **Νίγερ Níger, neeg'-er; of Latin origin; black; Niger, a Christian: Niger**. According to the African American Registry (2019): "The history of the word **nigger is often traced to the Latin word Niger, meaning Black**. This word became the noun, Negro (Black person) in English." The KJV bible book of Hosea, chapter 4 verse 6; states: "My people are destroyed for lack of knowledge: because thou hast rejected knowledge, I will also reject thee, that thou shalt be no priest to me: seeing thou hast forgotten the law of thy God, I will also forget thy children."

22

"And whatsoever we ask, we receive of him, because we keep his commandments, and do those things that are pleasing in his sight, KJV 1 John 3:22."

Beware of the Pink Assassin (Your Tongue): The True Vine (Yashu'a, Jesus) Power of Life and Death is in the Tongue;
Speaking God's (אלהים Elóhíym) "Will" for Your Life into Existence!

Oh, Gracious Most High Heavenly father, Holy is your name,
Your Will Be Done Now and Forever!

The KJV bible book of Isaiah, chapter 5 verse 13; states: "Therefore my people are gone into captivity, because they have no knowledge: and their honorable men are famished, and their multitude dried up with thirst." So, the Children of the Most High Pristine Youth and Family Solutions, LLC. refer to themselves as **Teachers** instead of **Preachers** because after over 25 years of teaching and studying the scriptures in the languages that they were originally revealed in, the children of the Most High don't find themselves **preaching**, they found themselves **teaching**. According to the Online American Heritage Dictionary, **teaching means; instructing, explaining, and elaborating**. So, we **teach** in an effort to ensure that the children of the Most High do their best to make the doctrine of the Most High clear in the minds of people who want to learn the original message or messages of the scriptures before they were translated into other languages.

23

"And whatsoever we ask, we receive of him, because we keep his commandments, and do those things that are pleasing in his sight, KJV 1 John 3:22."

Beware of the Pink Assassin (Your Tongue): The True Vine
(Yashu'a, Jesus) Power of Life and Death is in the Tongue;
**Speaking God's (אלהים Elohîym) "Will"
for Your Life into Existence!**

CHILDREN OF THE MOST HIGH:
PRISTINE YOUTH AND FAMILY SOLUTIONS, LLC.
SONS AND DAUGHTERS OF THE MOST HIGH PUBLISHERS ®

*Oh, Gracious Most High Heavenly father, Holy is your name,
Your Will Be Done Now and Forever!*

According to the Online American Heritage Dictionary (2020),

Administer is defined as:

ad·min·is·ter (ăd-mĭnꞏĭ-stər)

v. **ad·min·is·tered, ad·min·is·ter·ing, ad·min·is·ters**

v.tr.

1. To have charge of; manage.

2.a. To apply as a remedy: *administer a sedative.* **1.** To manage
as an administrator. **2.** To minister: *administering to their every
whim.* [Middle English *administren*, from Old French
administrer, from Latin *administrāre* : *ad*, ad- + *ministrāre*, to
manage (from *minister, ministr-*, servant; see <u>MINISTER</u>).]

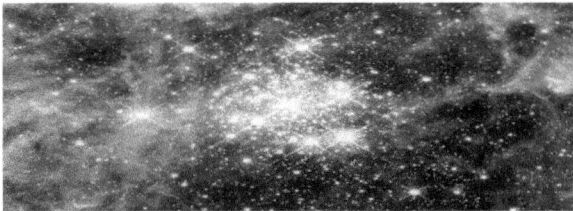

24

**"And whatsoever we ask, we receive of him,
because we keep his commandments, and do those
things that are pleasing in his sight, KJV 1 John 3:22."**

Beware of the Pink Assassin (Your Tongue): The True Vine (Yashu'a, Jesus) Power of Life and Death is in the Tongue;
Speaking God's (אלהים Elohîym) "Will" for Your Life into Existence!

CHILDREN OF THE MOST HIGH:
PRISTINE YOUTH AND FAMILY SOLUTIONS, LLC.
SONS AND DAUGHTERS OF THE MOST HIGH PUBLISHERS ®

Oh, Gracious Most High Heavenly father, Holy is your name,
Your Will Be Done Now and Forever!

So, we are **"Administers of the Most High's Doctrine"** by way of the Most High Heavenly Father giving the Children of the Most High: Pristine Youth and Family Solutions, LLC. **charge of managing the administering** of his Doctrine to inspire and empower all children of the Most High to pristinely make the world a safe and healthy place for all members of humanity. Which occurs by <u>applying the Doctrine of the Most High as a remedy to create a world that is ruled by Love and the "Will" of the Most High, void of negative emotions, greed, lusts and love of money</u>.

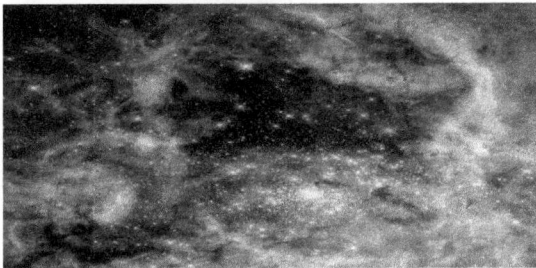

25

"And whatsoever we ask, we receive of him, because we keep his commandments, and do those things that are pleasing in his sight, KJV 1 John 3:22."

Beware of the Pink Assassin (Your Tongue): The True Vine
(Yashu'a, Jesus) Power of Life and Death is in the Tongue;
Speaking God's (אלהים Elôhîym) "Will"
for Your Life into Existence!

CHILDREN OF THE MOST HIGH:
PRISTINE YOUTH AND FAMILY SOLUTIONS, LLC.
SONS AND DAUGHTERS OF THE MOST HIGH PUBLISHERS ®

Oh, Gracious Most High Heavenly father, Holy is your name,
Your Will Be Done Now and Forever!

Why does the work that the Children of the Most High Pristine Youth and Family Solutions, LLC. do Matter?

In order for the Children of the Most High; Pristine Youth and Family Solutions LLC. to be obedient to the Most High Heavenly Father, we seek to be positive difference makers who helps and teach youth and adults how to apply the doctrine of the Most High through the **True Vine "Yashu'a" (Jesus) B.A.-K.A.-R.E. Sequential Order of Learning** to teach them how to create positive predetermined goals, how to achieve positive success according to what positive success means to them, how to achieve positive happiness according to what positive happiness means to them, and how to learn to work together with members of humanity to create a world where all youth and all adults are happy, healthy, and balanced mentally, spiritually, physically, emotionally, financially, personally, professionally, and socially.

26

"And whatsoever we ask, we receive of him,
because we keep his commandments, and do those
things that are pleasing in his sight, KJV 1 John 3:22."

Beware of the Pink Assassin (Your Tongue): The True Vine (Yashu'a, Jesus) Power of Life and Death is in the Tongue; Speaking God's (אלהים Elóhîym) "Will" for Your Life into Existence!

CHILDREN OF THE MOST HIGH:
PRISTINE YOUTH AND FAMILY SOLUTIONS, LLC.
SONS AND DAUGHTERS OF THE MOST HIGH PUBLISHERS ®

Oh, Gracious Most High Heavenly father, Holy is your name, Your Will Be Done Now and Forever!

"Happiness is associated with and precedes numerous successful outcomes, as well as behaviors paralleling success, Lyubomirsky, King, and Diener, (2005). Furthermore, the evidence suggests that positive affect is the hallmark of well-being and may be the cause of many of the desirable characteristics, resources, and successes correlated with happiness, (Lyubomirsky, King, & Diener, (2005)." It also matters for our youth to receive the protection from the Most High Heavenly Father from all harm during the pre-adult years and beyond, in order to have an opportunity to become adults that can continue to create a world where all youth and all adults are happy, healthy, and balanced mentally, spiritually, physically, emotionally, financially, personally, professionally, and socially.

27

"And whatsoever we ask, we receive of him, because we keep his commandments, and do those things that are pleasing in his sight, KJV 1 John 3:22."

Beware of the Pink Assassin (Your Tongue): The True Vine
(Yashu'a, Jesus) Power of Life and Death is in the Tongue;
Speaking God's (אלהים Elôhîym) "Will"
for Your Life into Existence!

CHILDREN OF THE MOST HIGH:
PRISTINE YOUTH AND FAMILY SOLUTIONS, LLC.
SONS AND DAUGHTERS OF THE MOST HIGH PUBLISHERS ®

Oh, Gracious Most High Heavenly father, Holy is your name,
Your Will Be Done Now and Forever!

According the bible, this can only occur if our youth learn God's knowledge and obey God's laws. In the KJV bible book of Hosea chapter 4 verse 6, the LORD states: "**My people are destroyed for lack of knowledge**: because thou hast rejected knowledge, I will also reject thee, that thou shalt be no priest to me: **seeing thou hast forgotten the law of thy God, I will also forget thy children**." So, according to the aforementioned verse, in order to best prepare today's youth to survive and thrive until adulthood and beyond, they need to learn **God's (אלהים Elôhîym) knowledge (Elôhîym, אלהים is the original word for "God" before being translated as the word: "God" in the KJV bible book of Genesis chapter 1 verse 1)**, and **God's (אלהים Elôhîym) laws to be eligible to receive God's (אלהים Elôhîym) protection from all harm.**

28
"And whatsoever we ask, we receive of him,
because we keep his commandments, and do those
things that are pleasing in his sight, KJV 1 John 3:22."

Beware of the Pink Assassin (Your Tongue): The True Vine (Yashu'a, Jesus) Power of Life and Death is in the Tongue; Speaking God's (אלהים Elôhîym) "Will" for Your Life into Existence!

CHILDREN OF THE MOST HIGH:
PRISTINE YOUTH AND FAMILY SOLUTIONS, LLC.
SONS AND DAUGHTERS OF THE MOST HIGH PUBLISHERS ®

Oh, Gracious Most High Heavenly father, Holy is your name,
Your Will Be Done Now and Forever!

Therefore, today's youth must be informed with **God's (אלהים Elôhîym) All, Wise, Abundant, Right, Exact (A.W.A.R.E.) Knowledge**. How do you know? Because God's **A.W.A.R.E.** knowledge is **bes**t, **accurate**, **correct** (**right, healthy)** and **exact** and best to guide and protect all of the global children of the Most High from all harm. For this reason, **God's (אלהים Elôhîym) A.W.A.R.E. Knowledge** gives the children of the Most High the ability to develop the habit of **positive thinking** or correct (**right, healthy) thinking** as oppose to **negative thinking** or **wrong thinking**. A person with **wrong knowledge** thinks negatively by having **wrong I. D. E. A. S. (I**mpure **D**esires **E**motionally **A**ctivated **S**equentially) or negative thoughts continuously, which leads to negative thinking, negative speaking, negative actions, and negative character.

29
"And whatsoever we ask, we receive of him,
because we keep his commandments, and do those
things that are pleasing in his sight, KJV 1 John 3:22."

Beware of the Pink Assassin (Your Tongue): The True Vine (Yashu'a, Jesus) Power of Life and Death is in the Tongue; Speaking God's (אלהים Elohîym) "Will" for Your Life into Existence!

CHILDREN OF THE MOST HIGH:
PRISTINE YOUTH AND FAMILY SOLUTIONS, LLC.
SONS AND DAUGHTERS OF THE MOST HIGH PUBLISHERS ®

Oh, Gracious Most High Heavenly father, Holy is your name, Your Will Be Done Now and Forever!

Learning, applying and obeying the laws of Elohiym (God), activates the will of the Most High Heavenly Father in the mind which initiates all thoughts, and a person acts and speaks, as he or she thinks! This is why in the KJV bible book of Hebrews chapter 8 verse 10; it states: "For this is the covenant that I will make with the house of Israel after those days, saith the Lord; **I will put my laws into their mind, and write them in their hearts**: and I will be to them a God, and they shall be to me a people."

30

"And whatsoever we ask, we receive of him, because we keep his commandments, and do those things that are pleasing in his sight, KJV 1 John 3:22."

Beware of the Pink Assassin (Your Tongue): The True Vine (Yashu'a, Jesus) Power of Life and Death is in the Tongue;
Speaking God's (אלהים Elohîym) "Will"
for Your Life into Existence!

CHILDREN OF THE MOST HIGH:
PRISTINE YOUTH AND FAMILY SOLUTIONS, LLC.
SONS AND DAUGHTERS OF THE MOST HIGH PUBLISHERS ®

Oh, Gracious Most High Heavenly father, Holy is your name,
Your Will Be Done Now and Forever!

In the KJV bible book of Revelation chapter 22 verses 12-16; Yashu'a (Jesus) stated: "**And, behold, I come quickly; and my reward is with me, to give every man according as his work shall be. I am Alpha and Omega, the beginning and the end, the first and the last. Blessed are they that do his** [the Most High, Heavenly Father's, **ELYOWN** עֶלְיוֹן **EL** אֵל] **commandments, that they may have right to the tree of life, and may enter in through the gates into the city. For without are dogs, and sorcerers, and whoremongers, and murderers, and idolaters, and whosoever loveth and maketh a lie. "I Jesus** [Yashu'a] **have sent mine angel to testify unto you these things in the churches. I am the root and the offspring of David, and the bright and morning star."**

31

"And whatsoever we ask, we receive of him, because we keep his commandments, and do those things that are pleasing in his sight, KJV 1 John 3:22."

Beware of the Pink Assassin (Your Tongue): The True Vine
(Yashu'a, Jesus) Power of Life and Death is in the Tongue;
Speaking God's (אלהים Elóhîym) "Will"
for Your Life into Existence!

*Oh, Gracious Most High Heavenly father, Holy is your name,
Your Will Be Done Now and Forever!*

Hence, **God's (אלהים Elôhîym) A.W.A.R.E. Knowledge** is the
best knowledge for our youth to be taught in order for them to
have the best opportunity to be recipients of **Elohiym** (God's)
protection, and to help ensure that our youth will become the
future positive leaders of tomorrow, today!

32

**"And whatsoever we ask, we receive of him,
because we keep his commandments, and do those
things that are pleasing in his sight, KJV 1 John 3:22."**

Beware of the Pink Assassin (Your Tongue): The True Vine (Yashu'a, Jesus) Power of Life and Death is in the Tongue;
Speaking God's (אלהים Elôhîym) "Will" for Your Life into Existence!

CHILDREN OF THE MOST HIGH:
PRISTINE YOUTH AND FAMILY SOLUTIONS, LLC.
SONS AND DAUGHTERS OF THE MOST HIGH PUBLISHERS ®

Oh, Gracious Most High Heavenly father, Holy is your name,
Your Will Be Done Now and Forever!

Introduction:

The Children of the Most High: Pristine Youth and Family Solutions, LLC. is putting forth this book entitled: "**Beware of the Pink Assassin (Your Tongue): The True Vine (Yashu'a, Jesus) Power of Life and Death is in the Tongue; Speaking God's (אלהים Elôhîym) "Will" for Your Life into Existence!** By the will of the Most High Heavenly Father to **inspire ALL youth and ALL adults who are children of the Most High learn how to best listen and how to best communicate through Love,** and **how to Only Speak through the portion of the Most High that exists in each of us**, like the **True-Vine (Yashu'a, Jesus)** did! According to the Online KJV Blue Letter bible Greek Strong's Concordance (2020), "the word "**power**" is mentioned **272** times in **260** verses."

33
"And whatsoever we ask, we receive of him, because we keep his commandments, and do those things that are pleasing in his sight, KJV 1 John 3:22."

Beware of the Pink Assassin (Your Tongue): The True Vine
(Yashu'a, Jesus) Power of Life and Death is in the Tongue;
Speaking God's (אלהים Eloh**î**ym) "Will"
for Your Life into Existence!

CHILDREN OF THE MOST HIGH:
PRISTINE YOUTH AND FAMILY SOLUTIONS, LLC.
SONS AND DAUGHTERS OF THE MOST HIGH PUBLISHERS ®

Oh, Gracious Most High Heavenly father, Holy is your name,
Your Will Be Done Now and Forever!

"The word the word "**life**" is mentioned **450** times in **409** verses.
The word "**death**" is mentioned **372** times in **342** verses. The
word "**tongue**" is mentioned **129** times in **126** verses. The word
"**word**" is mentioned **697** times in **673** verses. The word
"**speaketh**" is mentioned **74** times in **66** verses. The word
"**speak**" is mentioned **513** times in **484** verses. The word
"**mouth**" is mentioned **424** times in **397** verses. The word "**lips**"
is mentioned **119** times in **118** verses. The word "**ask**" is
mentioned **109** times in **103** verses. The words "**keep my
saying**" is mentioned **29** times in **8** verses. The word "**said**" is
mentioned **4,002** times in **3,605** verses. The words "**keep my
commandments**" is mentioned **92** times in **22** verses. The
words "**ask in my name**" is mentioned **27** times in **6** verses."
Therefore; **according to the KJV bible; the True Vine
(Yashu'a, Jesus) Power of Life and Death is in the Tongue,
words, keeping of sayings, keeping of commandments, and
how we speak matters!**

34
**"And whatsoever we ask, we receive of him,
because we keep his commandments, and do those
things that are pleasing in his sight, KJV 1 John 3:22."**

Beware of the Pink Assassin (Your Tongue): The True Vine (Yashu'a, Jesus) Power of Life and Death is in the Tongue; Speaking God's (אלהים Elŏhíym) "Will" for Your Life into Existence!

CHILDREN OF THE MOST HIGH:
PRISTINE YOUTH AND FAMILY SOLUTIONS, LLC.
SONS AND DAUGHTERS OF THE MOST HIGH PUBLISHERS ®

*Oh, Gracious Most High Heavenly father, Holy is your name,
Your Will Be Done Now and Forever!*

Sometimes our tongue, symbolically; writes checks (**saying things that are not best to say**); that the **Sowing and Reaping Bank can't cash**! So, we have to Beware (**Be Aware**) of the Pink Assassin (**Your Tongue**) because the True Vine (Yashu'a, Jesus) Power of Life and Death is in the Tongue. Therefore; **the children of the Most High must continuously put the following words in A.C.T.I.O.N. (Activated, Consciousness, Timely, Intentions, Obligated, Now) through all of our works, and in all that we are graciously blessed with the opportunity to do**: "On my own accord, I can of mine own self do nothing, I seek not mine own will, but the will of the Father which hath sent me" according to the Most High Heavenly Father's pre**ordained purpose** for your life." **By thinking, saying, and doing the aforementioned; you can be very successful at** Mind Gardening in the Creative Garden of Will (Your Mind) to grow the habit of speaking the True Vine (Yashu'a, Jesus) Power of Life INTO EXISTENCE by the "Will" of the Most High Heavenly Father for your life!

35

"And whatsoever we ask, we receive of him, because we keep his commandments, and do those things that are pleasing in his sight, KJV 1 John 3:22."

Beware of the Pink Assassin (Your Tongue): The True Vine
(Yashu'a, Jesus) Power of Life and Death is in the Tongue;
Speaking God's (אלהים Elohîym) "Will"
for Your Life into Existence!

Oh, Gracious Most High Heavenly father, Holy is your name,
Your Will Be Done Now and Forever!

Chapter 1: Beware of the Pink Assassin (Your Tongue): The True Vine (Yashu'a, Jesus) Power of Life and Death is in the Tongue!

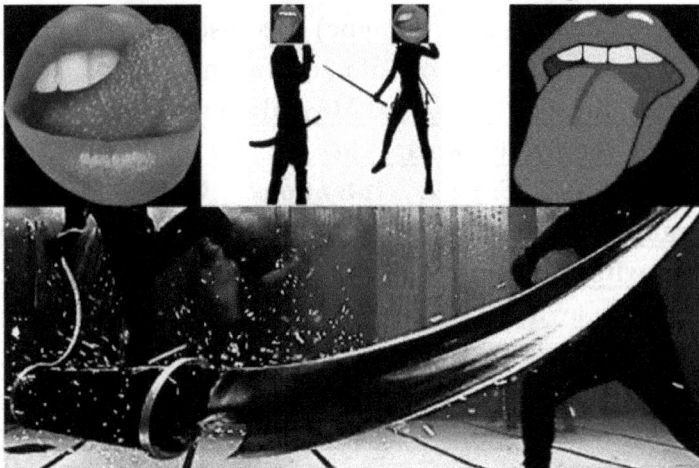

"**In the beginning was the Word, and the Word was with God, and the Word was God**, KJV John 1:1." "**Death and life are in the power of the tongue: and they that love it shall eat the fruit thereof**, KJV Proverbs 18:21."

36

"And whatsoever we ask, we receive of him, because we keep his commandments, and do those things that are pleasing in his sight, KJV 1 John 3:22."

Beware of the Pink Assassin (Your Tongue): The True Vine (Yashu'a, Jesus) Power of Life and Death is in the Tongue; Speaking God's (אלהים Elŏhîym) "Will" for Your Life into Existence!

CHILDREN OF THE MOST HIGH:
PRISTINE YOUTH AND FAMILY SOLUTIONS, LLC.
SONS AND DAUGHTERS OF THE MOST HIGH PUBLISHERS ®

Oh, Gracious Most High Heavenly father, Holy is your name, Your Will Be Done Now and Forever!

Explain the aforementioned KJV bible book of John chapter 1 verse 1? According to the Online KJV Blue Letter bible Greek Strong's Concordance (2020), "**In** (ἐν **En**) **the beginning** (ἀρχή **Archē**) **was** the **Word** (λόγος **Logos**), and the **Word** (λόγος **Logos**) was **with** (πρός **Pros**) **God** (θεός **Theos**), and the **Word** (λόγος **Logos**) was (ἦν **ēn**) **God**." The KJV bible Greek Strong's Concordance (2020), **#1722** is the word for (**In**): ἐν **En (pronounced as en)**, and is defined as: **a primary preposition denoting (fixed) position (in place, time or state**). The KJV bible Greek Strong's Concordance #**746** is the word for (**beginning**): ἀρχή **Archē (pronounced as Ar-Khay'**), and is defined as: **beginning, origin, that by which anything begins to be, the origin, the active cause**."

37

"And whatsoever we ask, we receive of him, because we keep his commandments, and do those things that are pleasing in his sight, KJV 1 John 3:22."

CHILDREN OF THE MOST HIGH:
PRISTINE YOUTH AND FAMILY SOLUTIONS, LLC.
SONS AND DAUGHTERS OF THE MOST HIGH PUBLISHERS ®

Oh, Gracious Most High Heavenly father, Holy is your name,
Your Will Be Done Now and Forever!

The KJV bible Greek Strong's Concordance (2020), "**#2258** is the word for (**was**): ἦν ēn (**pronounced as Ane**), defined as: **was**." According to the Online Thayer KJV Bible Lexicon (2011), the KJV bible Greek Strong's Concordance "**#3056** is the word for (**Word**): λόγος **Logos**, defined as: properly, a collecting, collection (**see λέγω**) — and that, **as well of those things which are put together in thought**, **as of those which, having been thought, gathered together in the mind, are expressed in words**. **Accordingly, a twofold use of the term is to be distinguished: one which relates to speaking, and one which relates to thinking**. I. **As respects speech**: 1. **a word, yet not in the grammatical sense**, **a word which, uttered by the living voice, embodies a conception or idea**; to utter a distinct word, intelligible speech, to speak a word against, to the injury of, one, to drive out demons."

38

"And whatsoever we ask, we receive of him, because we keep his commandments, and do those things that are pleasing in his sight, KJV 1 John 3:22."

Beware of the Pink Assassin (Your Tongue): The True Vine (Yashu'a, Jesus) Power of Life and Death is in the Tongue; Speaking God's (אלהים Elóhîym) "Will" for Your Life into Existence!

CHILDREN OF THE MOST HIGH:
PRISTINE YOUTH AND FAMILY SOLUTIONS, LLC.
SONS AND DAUGHTERS OF THE MOST HIGH PUBLISHERS ®

Oh, Gracious Most High Heavenly father, Holy is your name,
Your Will Be Done Now and Forever!

"**Of the words of a conversation**, 2. what someone has said; a saying; b. **of the sayings of God**; **equivalent to decree, mandate, order**: β. **of the moral precepts given by God in the O. T.** γ. **equivalent to promise**: **universally, a divine declaration recorded in the O. T., John 12:38; John 15:25; 1 Corinthians 15:54. Through prayer in which the language of the O. T. is employed**: Often in the O. T. prophets, "an oracle or utterance by which God discloses, to the prophets or through the prophets, future events": used collectively of the sum of such utterances, Revelation 1:2, 9; c. **what is declared, a thought**, **declaration**, **aphorism**: **a dictum, maxim or weighty saying**: **equivalent to proverb**. 3. **Discourse, the act of speaking**, **speech**: **equivalent to the faculty of speech**: **skill and practice in speaking**."

"And whatsoever we ask, we receive of him, because we keep his commandments, and do those things that are pleasing in his sight, KJV 1 John 3:22."

Beware of the Pink Assassin (Your Tongue): The True Vine
(Yashu'a, Jesus) Power of Life and Death is in the Tongue;
**Speaking God's (אלהים Elohîym) "Will"
for Your Life into Existence!**

*Oh, Gracious Most High Heavenly father, Holy is your name,
Your Will Be Done Now and Forever!*

"<u>The art of speaking to the purpose about things pertaining
to wisdom or knowledge</u>, c. <u>a kind (or style) of speaking</u>:
utterance from God, continuous speaking, discourse, e.
instruction: <u>concerning this salvation (the salvation
obtained through Christ</u>), **the first instruction concerning
Christ. 4. <u>in an objective sense, what is communicated by
instruction, doctrine: universally</u>, <u>the doctrines of faith</u>,
<u>specifically, the doctrine concerning the attainment through
Christ of salvation in the kingdom of God</u>. 1. reason, <u>the
mental faculty of thinking, meditating, reasoning,
calculating, etc.</u>, <u>of the divine mind</u>**, pervading and noting all
things by its proper force. 2. account, i. e. regard, consideration:
to have regard for, make account of a thing. 3. account, i. e.
reckoning, score, to your account, to your advantage, to make a
reckoning, settle accounts."

40

**"And whatsoever we ask, we receive of him,
because we keep his commandments, and do those
things that are pleasing in his sight, KJV 1 John 3:22."**

Beware of the Pink Assassin (Your Tongue): The True Vine
(Yashu'a, Jesus) Power of Life and Death is in the Tongue;
Speaking God's (אלהים Elóhîym) "Will"
for Your Life into Existence!

CHILDREN OF THE MOST HIGH:
PRISTINE YOUTH AND FAMILY SOLUTIONS, LLC.
SONS AND DAUGHTERS OF THE MOST HIGH PUBLISHERS ®

Oh, Gracious Most High Heavenly father, Holy is your name,
Your Will Be Done Now and Forever!

"4. account, answer or explanation in reference to judgment, to give or render an account. 5. relation, with whom as judge we have to do, as is right, justly. 6. reason, cause, ground, for what reason? why? III. In several passages in the writings of John denotes **the essential Word of God, the power in union with God, his minister in the creation and government of the universe, the cause of all the world's life both physical and spiritually, which for the procurement of man's salvation put on human nature in the person of Jesus the Messiah and shone forth conspicuously from his words and deeds**."

41

"And whatsoever we ask, we receive of him, because we keep his commandments, and do those things that are pleasing in his sight, KJV 1 John 3:22."

CHILDREN OF THE MOST HIGH:
PRISTINE YOUTH AND FAMILY SOLUTIONS, LLC.
SONS AND DAUGHTERS OF THE MOST HIGH PUBLISHERS ®

Oh, Gracious Most High Heavenly father, Holy is your name, Your Will Be Done Now and Forever!

According to the KJV bible Greek Strong's Concordance (2020), **#3056** is the word for (**Word**): λόγος **Logos**, defined as: **reasoning (the mental faculty), the Divine Expression (Christ)**, of speech, a word uttered by a living voice, embodies a conception or idea, what someone has said, a word, **the sayings of God, decree, mandate or order, of the moral precepts given by God**, Old Testament prophecy given by the prophets, **what is declared**, a thought, **declaration, aphorism, a weighty saying, a dictum, a maxim, discourse, the act of speaking, speech, the faculty of speech**, skill and practice in speaking, a kind or style of speaking, a continuous speaking discourse – **instruction, doctrine**, teaching, **its use as respect to the MIND alone**, reason, **the mental faculty of thinking, meditating, reasoning**, calculating, account, regard, consideration, reckoning, score."

42

"And whatsoever we ask, we receive of him, because we keep his commandments, and do those things that are pleasing in his sight, KJV 1 John 3:22."

Beware of the Pink Assassin (Your Tongue): The True Vine (Yashu'a, Jesus) Power of Life and Death is in the Tongue;
Speaking God's (אלהים Elŏhîym) "Will"
for Your Life into Existence!

*Oh, Gracious Most High Heavenly father, Holy is your name,
Your Will Be Done Now and Forever!*

"Answer or explanation in reference to judgment, relation, with whom as judge we stand in relation, reason, cause, ground. **In John, denotes the essential Word of God, Jesus Christ, the personal wisdom and power in union with God, his minister in creation and government of the universe, the cause of all the world's life both physical and spiritually**, which for the procurement of **human beings salvation put on human nature in the person of Jesus the Messiah**."

43

"And whatsoever we ask, we receive of him, because we keep his commandments, and do those things that are pleasing in his sight, KJV 1 John 3:22."

Beware of the Pink Assassin (Your Tongue): The True Vine
(Yashu'a, Jesus) Power of Life and Death is in the Tongue;
**Speaking God's (אלהים Elóhîym) "Will"
for Your Life into Existence!**

*Oh, Gracious Most High Heavenly father, Holy is your name,
Your Will Be Done Now and Forever!*

In the aforementioned KJV bible Greek Strong's Concordance
(2020), thorough explanation of the KJV bible book John
chapter 1 verse 1; when it says: "**In the beginning (ἀρχή
Archē) was the word for (Word): λόγος Logos**, defined as:
**reasoning (the mental faculty), the Divine Expression
(Christ)**, of speech, **a word uttered by a living voice**,
doctrine, **teaching**, **its use as respect to the MIND alone**,
reason, **the mental faculty of thinking**, **meditating;**" is there
a correlation with the Messiah being before Abraham, and
Genesis chapter 1 verses 1 and 2?

44

**"And whatsoever we ask, we receive of him,
because we keep his commandments, and do those
things that are pleasing in his sight, KJV 1 John 3:22."**

Beware of the Pink Assassin (Your Tongue): The True Vine
(Yashu'a, Jesus) Power of Life and Death is in the Tongue;
Speaking God's (אלהים Elơhîym) "Will"
for Your Life into Existence!

CHILDREN OF THE MOST HIGH:
PRISTINE YOUTH AND FAMILY SOLUTIONS, LLC.
SONS AND DAUGHTERS OF THE MOST HIGH PUBLISHERS ®

*Oh, Gracious Most High Heavenly father, Holy is your name,
Your Will Be Done Now and Forever!*

In the KJV bible book of John chapter 8 verse 58, **the Messiah
Yashu'a (Jesus) said: "Verily (ἀμήν Amēn), verily (ἀμήν
Amēn), I say unto you, Before Abraham was, I am." How
did the Messiah Yashu'a (Jesus) exist in the beginning (ἀρχή
Archē pronounced as Ar-Khay') of the KJV bible if he was
not born until sometime in the New Testament**? According
to the KJV bible book of John chapter 1 verse 14, and Matthew
chapter 2 verse 1; it states: "And **the Word was made flesh
(σάρξ Sarx – pronounced as: Sä'rks and means: human flesh
(the soft substance of the living body, which covers the
bones and is permeated with blood, the body of a man)**, and
dwelt among us, (and we beheld his glory, the glory as of the
only begotten of the Father,) full of grace and truth. Now when
Jesus was born in **Bethlehem** (Βηθλέεμ Bēthleem –
pronounced as: **Ba-thle'-em** and means: "**House of Bread**" The
Messiah Yashu'a (Jesus) said that: "I AM the Living Bread)"
of Judaea in the days of Herod the king, behold, there came wise
men from the east to Jerusalem."

45

**"And whatsoever we ask, we receive of him,
because we keep his commandments, and do those
things that are pleasing in his sight, KJV 1 John 3:22."**

CHILDREN OF THE MOST HIGH:
PRISTINE YOUTH AND FAMILY SOLUTIONS, LLC.
SONS AND DAUGHTERS OF THE MOST HIGH PUBLISHERS ®

Oh, Gracious Most High Heavenly father, Holy is your name,
Your Will Be Done Now and Forever!

In the KJV bible book of John chapter 6 verse 51; the Messiah Yashu'a (Jesus) said: "<u>I am the living bread</u> which came down from heaven: if any man (τις **Tis – which means a male or female person**) eat of this bread, he [**or she**] shall live forever: and the bread that I will give is my flesh, which I will give for the life of the world. The KJV bible book of Genesis chapter 1 verses 1-2 states: "**In the beginning** God created the heaven and the earth. And the earth was without form, and void; and darkness was upon the face of the deep. And **the Spirit of God** moved upon the face of the waters." The KJV bible book of John chapter 1 verses 1-3 states: "**In the beginning** was **the Word**, and **the Word** was **with God**, **and the Word was God**. **The same was in the beginning with God**. **All things were made by him; and without him was not anything made that was made**."

46

"And whatsoever we ask, we receive of him, because we keep his commandments, and do those things that are pleasing in his sight, KJV 1 John 3:22."

Beware of the Pink Assassin (Your Tongue): The True Vine (Yashu'a, Jesus) Power of Life and Death is in the Tongue; Speaking God's (אלהים Elôhîym) "Will" for Your Life into Existence!

CHILDREN OF THE MOST HIGH:
PRISTINE YOUTH AND FAMILY SOLUTIONS, LLC.
SONS AND DAUGHTERS OF THE MOST HIGH PUBLISHERS ®

Oh, Gracious Most High Heavenly father, Holy is your name,
Your Will Be Done Now and Forever!

So, the Messiah Yashu'a (Jesus) was **in the beginning as one with God or one with ALL in Spirit** in Genesis chapter 1 before Abraham. The Messiah Yashu'a (Jesus) also exists before Abraham as the **Spirit of God**. When God (אלהים Elôhîym) sends "**the Spirit of God**" to earth, **the word and the spirit** became flesh as the Messiah Yashu'a (Jesus) in the New Testament of the bible. The Most High Heavenly Father's **thought** of "**the Word**," came **INTO EXISTENCE, and "the Word became flesh**," by the "Will" of the Most High Heavenly Father. "And **the LORD said, My spirit** shall not always strive **with man** (**a human being, singular**), for that he also **is flesh**: yet his days shall be a hundred and twenty years, KJV Genesis 6:3."

47

"And whatsoever we ask, we receive of him, because we keep his commandments, and do those things that are pleasing in his sight, KJV 1 John 3:22."

Beware of the Pink Assassin (Your Tongue): The True Vine (Yashu'a, Jesus) Power of Life and Death is in the Tongue;
**Speaking God's (אלהים Elohîym) "Will"
for Your Life into Existence!**

CHILDREN OF THE MOST HIGH:
PRISTINE YOUTH AND FAMILY SOLUTIONS, LLC.
SONS AND DAUGHTERS OF THE MOST HIGH PUBLISHERS ®

*Oh, Gracious Most High Heavenly father, Holy is your name,
Your Will Be Done Now and Forever!*

What does the word "Genesis" mean? The translated word "Genesis" is from the **Greek word GHEN-NAY-SIS** meaning: "the very beginning." **Why would an Aramic/Hebrew bible have translated Greek names for their chapters if those translated chapters were not influenced by the Greeks**? **And is it possible that the Greek influences on an Aramic/Hebrew bible, may have been inclusive of some bias?** The word **"Genesis"** is **Ghen'nay-Sis**, from **Genos, Ghen-Os**, meaning: **particular kind or kindred**; **Gennao** means: **"To Procreate"** of a father by extension of a mother, the word **Genealogia** and **Genealogeo** means: **"Tracing by Generations"**, making **Genesis a book of Generations."**

48

"And whatsoever we ask, we receive of him, because we keep his commandments, and do those things that are pleasing in his sight, KJV 1 John 3:22."

Beware of the Pink Assassin (Your Tongue): The True Vine (Yashu'a, Jesus) Power of Life and Death is in the Tongue; Speaking God's (אלהים Elohîym) "Will" for Your Life into Existence!

CHILDREN OF THE MOST HIGH:
PRISTINE YOUTH AND FAMILY SOLUTIONS, LLC.
SONS AND DAUGHTERS OF THE MOST HIGH PUBLISHERS ®

Oh, Gracious Most High Heavenly father, Holy is your name,
Your Will Be Done Now and Forever!

In the KJV book of the bible **Genesis chapter 2 verse 4**; it states with Hebrew inserts: **2:4** אֵלֶּה תוֹלְדוֹת הַשָּׁמַיִם וְהָאָרֶץ בְּהִבָּרְאָם בְּיוֹם עֲשׂוֹת יְהוָה אֱלֹהִים אֶרֶץ וְשָׁמָיִם:

"These אֵלֶּה 'El-leh are <u>the generations תּוֹלְדוֹת Towlĕdah of the heavens שָׁמַיִם Shamayim and of the earth אֶרֶץ 'Erets</u> when they were created בָּרָא Bara' (means Re-Create) (خلق) **(Khalaqa means Created, Procreated for the first time) in the day** יוֹם **Yowm that the Yĕhovah** יְהוָה **LORD Elohiym** אֱלֹהִים **God made** עָשָׂה `**Asah the earth** אֶרֶץ '**Erets and the heavens** שָׁמַיִם **Shamayim." So, the Most High Heavenly Father <u>Creates</u> (Khalaqa), and the Messiah Yashu'a <u>Makes</u> (**עָשָׂה** `**Asah in Aramic (Hebrew) and (γίνομαι Ginomai – make or made) in Greek."**

49

"And whatsoever we ask, we receive of him, because we keep his commandments, and do those things that are pleasing in his sight, KJV 1 John 3:22."

Speaking God's (אלהים Elŏhîym) "Will"
for Your Life into Existence!

CHILDREN OF THE MOST HIGH:
PRISTINE YOUTH AND FAMILY SOLUTIONS, LLC.
SONS AND DAUGHTERS OF THE MOST HIGH PUBLISHERS ®

Oh, Gracious Most High Heavenly father, Holy is your name,
Your Will Be Done Now and Forever!

The **Aramic/Hebrew** word: "תּוֹלְדוֹת Towlĕdah" is the KJV
bible Hebrew Strong's Concordance (2020), "**#8435**, and it
means: birth, descendants, results, proceedings, generations,
genealogies, account of men and their descendants,
genealogical list of one's descendants, one's contemporaries,
course of history (of creation), begetting in reference to
replenishment, not creation; of the generations or births of the
heavens and the earth.

תּוֹלְדֹת f. pl. (from the root יָלַד)—(1) *genera-*
tions, families, races, Nu. 1:20, seqq. לְתוֹלְדֹתָם
according to their races, Gen. 10:32; 25:13; Exod.
6:16. Hence סֵפֶר תּוֹלְדֹת genealogy, pedigree, Gen.
5:1. As a very large portion of the most ancient
Oriental history consists of genealogies, it means—
  (2) *history*, properly of families. Gen. 6:9, אֵלֶּה
תּוֹלְדֹת נֹחַ "this is the history of Noah." Genesis
37:2; and thus also applied to the *origin* of other
things. Gen. 2:4, " this is the origin of the heaven
and earth." (Compare יַחַשׂ and Syr. ܬܘܠܕܐ family,
genealogy, history.)

50

**"And whatsoever we ask, we receive of him,
because we keep his commandments, and do those
things that are pleasing in his sight, KJV 1 John 3:22."**

Beware of the Pink Assassin (Your Tongue): The True Vine (Yashu'a, Jesus) Power of Life and Death is in the Tongue; Speaking God's (אלהים Elóhîym) "Will" for Your Life into Existence!

CHILDREN OF THE MOST HIGH:
PRISTINE YOUTH AND FAMILY SOLUTIONS, LLC.
SONS AND DAUGHTERS OF THE MOST HIGH PUBLISHERS ®

Oh, Gracious Most High Heavenly father, Holy is your name,
Your Will Be Done Now and Forever!

What is the difference between the **original Aramic/Hebrew** words: **Barashiyth** or **Barasheeth** or **Rashiyth** or **Ray-Sheeth** and **Khalaqa**? The Original Aramic (Hebrew) name of the 1st Book of the Bible is: "**Barashiyth**" sometimes spelled: "**Rashiyth or Ray-Sheeth**" and in Aramic/Hebrew, it means: "**Re-Create, Pro-Create, Re-Construction, not to be confused with the original Aramic/Hebrew word: "Khalaqa"** which means **creation or creation period**. In the **Ashuric Syriac (Arabic)**, the word: "**Khalaq**" means **to create**. In the **Aramic/Hebrew** language, the word: "**Genesis**" is "**Barashiyth** or **Barasheeth**" is from the root word: "**Bara**" and means: "To **re**construct or **re**construction" not to be confused with the **original Aramic/Hebrew word: "Khalaqa"** which means **creation or creation period**."

51

"And whatsoever we ask, we receive of him, because we keep his commandments, and do those things that are pleasing in his sight, KJV 1 John 3:22."

Beware of the Pink Assassin (Your Tongue): The True Vine
(Yashu'a, Jesus) Power of Life and Death is in the Tongue;
Speaking God's (אלהים Elohîym) "Will"
for Your Life into Existence!

CHILDREN OF THE MOST HIGH:
PRISTINE YOUTH AND FAMILY SOLUTIONS, LLC.
SONS AND DAUGHTERS OF THE MOST HIGH PUBLISHERS ®

*Oh, Gracious Most High Heavenly father, Holy is your name,
Your Will Be Done Now and Forever!*

Barasheeth (בראשית) Comes From The Root Word Roshe (ראש)
Meaning *"The Head, Beginning, Captain, Chief, First, Forefront"*.

In the KJV bible book of Proverbs chapter 8 verse 23 with Hebrew inserts; it states: **8:23** מֵעוֹלָם נִסַּכְתִּי מֵרֹאשׁ מִקַּדְמֵי־אָרֶץ:

"I was set up נָסַךְ **Nacak** from everlasting עוֹלָם `**Owlam** from the **beginning** רֹאשׁ **Ro'she** or ever קֶדֶם **Qedem** the earth אֶרֶץ **'Erets** was." In the English language, the prefix: "**Re**" means to do again in comparison from the original Aramic (Hebrew) name of the 1st Book of the Bible is: "**Barashiyth**" from the root word: **Bara** which means: "**Re-construction**" and does not mean **"Khalaqa"**, which is the **original Aramic/Hebrew** word that means **creation or creation period."**

52
**"And whatsoever we ask, we receive of him,
because we keep his commandments, and do those
things that are pleasing in his sight, KJV 1 John 3:22."**

Beware of the Pink Assassin (Your Tongue): The True Vine (Yashu'a, Jesus) Power of Life and Death is in the Tongue; Speaking God's (אלהים Elohîym) "Will" for Your Life into Existence!

CHILDREN OF THE MOST HIGH:
PRISTINE YOUTH AND FAMILY SOLUTIONS, LLC.
SONS AND DAUGHTERS OF THE MOST HIGH PUBLISHERS ®

*Oh, Gracious Most High Heavenly father, Holy is your name,
Your Will Be Done Now and Forever!*

In the KJV bible book of Genesis chapter 1 verse 28 with Hebrew inserts; it states: **1:28** וַיְבָרֶךְ אֹתָם אֱלֹהִים וַיֹּאמֶר לָהֶם אֱלֹהִים פְּרוּ וּרְבוּ וּמִלְאוּ אֶת־הָאָרֶץ וְכִבְשֻׁהָ וּרְדוּ בִּדְגַת הַיָּם וּבְעוֹף הַשָּׁמַיִם וּבְכָל־חַיָּה הָרֹמֶשֶׂת עַל־הָאָרֶץ:

"And **Elohiym** אֱלֹהִים God blessed them בָּרַךְ **Barak** and **Elohiym** אֱלֹהִים God said אָמַר **'Amar** unto them, be fruitful פָּרָה **Parah** and multiply רָבָה **Rabah** and <u>replenish</u> מָלֵא <u>**Maw-lay'**</u> the earth אֶרֶץ **'Erets** and subdue it כָּבַשׁ **Kabash** and have dominion רָדָה **Radah** over the fish דָּגָה **Dagah** of the sea יָם **Yam** and over the fowl עוֹף `**Owph** of the air שָׁמַיִם **Shamayim** and over every living thing חַי **Khay or Chay** that moveth רָמַשׂ **Ramas** upon the earth אֶרֶץ **'Erets**. And God blessed them, and God said unto them, be fruitful, and multiply, and "**re-plenish**" the earth, and subdue it: and have dominion over the fish of the sea, and over the fowl of the air, and over every living thing that moveth upon the earth."

53

"And whatsoever we ask, we receive of him, because we keep his commandments, and do those things that are pleasing in his sight, KJV 1 John 3:22."

Beware of the Pink Assassin (Your Tongue): The True Vine (Yashu'a, Jesus) Power of Life and Death is in the Tongue; Speaking God's (אלהים Elohíym) "Will" for Your Life into Existence!

CHILDREN OF THE MOST HIGH:
PRISTINE YOUTH AND FAMILY SOLUTIONS, LLC.
SONS AND DAUGHTERS OF THE MOST HIGH PUBLISHERS ®

Oh, Gracious Most High Heavenly father, Holy is your name, Your Will Be Done Now and Forever!

The Aramic/Hebrew word used for **re-plenish** in the King James Version of the bible is the word is: "**MAW-LAY**" which means to **Re-Plenish** or **Re-Fill**: **For example:** If you were at a restaurant and you had a very good tasting lemonade that you drank up, you may ask the waiter or waitress if you can have a **Re-fill** on your lemonade. You can't **re-fill** or **re-plenish** something that was not already once filled or plenish. According to the KJV bible book of Genesis chapter 1 verse 28, Adam and Eve had to **re-fill** or **re-plenish** the earth (Genesis 1:28).

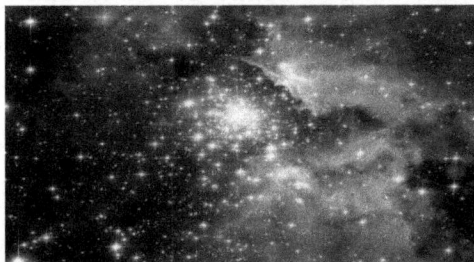

54

"And whatsoever we ask, we receive of him, because we keep his commandments, and do those things that are pleasing in his sight, KJV 1 John 3:22."

Beware of the Pink Assassin (Your Tongue): The True Vine
(Yashu'a, Jesus) Power of Life and Death is in the Tongue;
Speaking God's (אלהים Elŏhîym) "Will"
for Your Life into Existence!

CHILDREN OF THE MOST HIGH:
PRISTINE YOUTH AND FAMILY SOLUTIONS, LLC.
SONS AND DAUGHTERS OF THE MOST HIGH PUBLISHERS ®

Oh, Gracious Most High Heavenly father, Holy is your name,
Your Will Be Done Now and Forever!

So, in the KJV bible book of John chapter 1 verses 1-14, "**John, denotes the essential Word of God, the Messiah Yashu'a (Jesus Christ), the personal wisdom and power in union with God, his minister in creation and government of the universe, the cause of all the world's life both physical and spiritually**, which for the procurement of **human beings salvation put on human nature in the person of Jesus the Messiah**, Blue Letter KJV Greek Strong's Concordance, 2020."

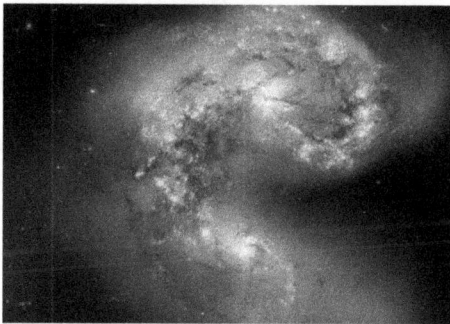

55

"And whatsoever we ask, we receive of him,
because we keep his commandments, and do those
things that are pleasing in his sight, KJV 1 John 3:22."

**Speaking God's (אלהים Elohîym) "Will"
for Your Life into Existence!**

CHILDREN OF THE MOST HIGH:
PRISTINE YOUTH AND FAMILY SOLUTIONS, LLC.
SONS AND DAUGHTERS OF THE MOST HIGH PUBLISHERS ®

*Oh, Gracious Most High Heavenly father, Holy is your name,
Your Will Be Done Now and Forever!*

**Explain the KJV bible book of Proverbs chapter 18 verse
21?** It states: "**Death and life are in the power of the tongue**:
and **they that love it** shall eat the **fruit** thereof)." According to
the Online KJV Blue Letter bible Greek Strong's Concordance
(2020), "**# 4194 is** מָוֶת **Maveth (pronounced as: Mä'·veth)** for
the word: "**Death**." מָוֶת **Maveth** is defined as: **death** (natural or
violent); concretely, the dead, their place or state (hades);
figuratively, pestilence, ruin: **(be) dead(-ly), death, die(-d)**. #
2416 is חַי **Khay or Chay** for the word: "**life**" (pronounced as:
Hayy or **Khah'-ee**). חַי **Khay or Chay** is defined as: alive, life.
 # 3027 is יָד **Yod or Yad (pronounced as: Yawd)**. יָד **Yod or
Yad** is defined as: **all manifested power of the hand** (the open
one indicating power, means, direction), **(be) able**, **thine own**,
power, **order**, and **ordinance**."

56
**"And whatsoever we ask, we receive of him,
because we keep his commandments, and do those
things that are pleasing in his sight, KJV 1 John 3:22."**

Beware of the Pink Assassin (Your Tongue): The True Vine (Yashu'a, Jesus) Power of Life and Death is in the Tongue; Speaking God's (אלהים Elohîym) "Will" for Your Life into Existence!

CHILDREN OF THE MOST HIGH:
PRISTINE YOUTH AND FAMILY SOLUTIONS, LLC.
SONS AND DAUGHTERS OF THE MOST HIGH PUBLISHERS ®

Oh, Gracious Most High Heavenly father, Holy is your name,
Your Will Be Done Now and Forever!

"# **3956** is לָשׁוֹן **Lashown** for the word: "**tongue**" (pronounced as: **Law-shone**). לָשׁוֹן **Lashown** is defined as: <u>the tongue of a person</u> or animals, **used literally as the instrument of** licking, eating, or **speech**), **and figuratively (speech, an ingot, a fork of flame, a cove of water):** babbler, bay, evil speaker, language, talker, wedge. #157 is אָהַב **'âhab** (pronounced as **aw-hab'**, ä·hav'). אָהַב **'âhab** is defined as: human appetite for objects such as food, drink, sleep, wisdom, <u>**human love for or to God**</u>, act of being a friend, lover (participle), **friend (participle) to righteousness**, like, friend."

אָהַב **'âhab** is also defined as:

57

"And whatsoever we ask, we receive of him,
because we keep his commandments, and do those
things that are pleasing in his sight, KJV 1 John 3:22."

Beware of the Pink Assassin (Your Tongue): The True Vine (Yashu'a, Jesus) Power of Life and Death is in the Tongue;

Speaking God's (אלהים Elohîym) "Will" for Your Life into Existence!

CHILDREN OF THE MOST HIGH:
PRISTINE YOUTH AND FAMILY SOLUTIONS, LLC.
SONS AND DAUGHTERS OF THE MOST HIGH PUBLISHERS ®

Oh, Gracious Most High Heavenly father, Holy is your name,
Your Will Be Done Now and Forever!

אָהַב & אָהֵב fut. יֶאֱהַב and יֶאֱהַב; 1 pers. אֹהַב Pro. 8:17; and אֹהַב Hos. 14:5; inf. אֱהֹב Ecc. 3:8 and אַהֲבָה.

(1) TO DESIRE, TO BREATHE AFTER anything. (The signification of breathing after, hence of longing, is proper to the syllables הב, חב, and with the letters softened, או, אב, comp. the roots חָבַב, הָבַל,

‌ to desire, to love; אָנָה and אָבָה to breathe after, to be inclined.) Construed with an accusative, Ps. 40:17; 70:5, seq.; לְ Ps. 116:1.

(2) *to love* (in which signification it accords with עָגַב ἀγαπάω), construed with an acc. Gen. 37:3, 4; Deu. 4:37; more rarely with לְ Lev. 19:18, 34, and בְּ Ecc. 5:9; 1 Sa. 20:17, אֲהֵבַת נַפְשֹׁו אֲהֵבֹו "he loved him as his own soul." Part. אֹהֵב *a friend,* i.e. one who is loving and beloved, intimate; different from רֵעַ a companion, Pro. 18:24; Est. 5:10, 14; Isa. 41:8, זֶרַע אַבְרָהָם אֹהֲבִי " the seed of Abraham my friend."

(3) *to delight* in anything, in doing anything; construed with a gerund of the verb; Hos. 12:8, לַעֲשֹׁק אָהֵב "he delights in oppression," or to oppress; Isa. 56:10; Jer. 14:10.

NIPHAL part. נֶאֱהָב *to be loved, amiable,* 2 Sam. 1:23.

PIEL part. מְאַהֵב.—(1) *a friend,* Zec. 13:6.

(2) *a lover,* especially in a bad sense; one given to licentious intercourse, a debauchee, Eze. 16:33, seq.; 23:5, seq. Always thus used, metaph. of idolaters. [Hence the following words.]

(related entry)

אָבַב a root unused in Hebrew. In Chaldee, in Pael אַבֵּב to produce fruit, especially the first and early fruit; Syr. ܐܒܒ to produce flowers. It appears in Arab., as well as in Heb., to have signified *to be verdant, to germinate;* see the derivatives אֵב greenness, אָבִיב ear of corn. I consider the primary sense to have been that of putting forth, protruding, germinating with impetus, shooting forth; Germ. treiben, whence אֵב junger Trieb, young shoots; so that it is kindred to the roots אָבָה, יָאַב, אָהַב, having the sense of desire, eager pursuit of an object; see אָהַב.

"And whatsoever we ask, we receive of him, because we keep his commandments, and do those things that are pleasing in his sight, KJV 1 John 3:22."

Beware of the Pink Assassin (Your Tongue): The True Vine (Yashu'a, Jesus) Power of Life and Death is in the Tongue; Speaking God's (אלהים Elŏhîym) "Will" for Your Life into Existence!

CHILDREN OF THE MOST HIGH:
PRISTINE YOUTH AND FAMILY SOLUTIONS, LLC.
SONS AND DAUGHTERS OF THE MOST HIGH PUBLISHERS ®

Oh, Gracious Most High Heavenly father, Holy is your name,
Your Will Be Done Now and Forever!

The KJV bible Greek Strong's Concordance "**#6529** is the word פְּרִי **Periy** for (**fruit**): פְּרִי **Periy** (**pronounced as: Per-ee'**). פְּרִי **Periy** is defined as: **fruit**, fruit produce (of the ground), fruit, **offspring, children, progeny (of the womb)**, **actions**." So, according to the aforementioned, "In the **beginning** (ἀρχή **Archē**) was **the Word** (λόγος **Logos**)" is a **Declaration of Faith**. "**The Word** (λόγος **Logos**) **of God** (θεός **Theos**)" is the divine mind creation and governing of the boundless universes, that caused of all the world's life both physical and spiritually to exist, and created the possibility of eternal salvation for human beings by way of the Most High Heavenly Father sending humanity salvation that put on the human nature in the person of Messiah Yashu'a (Jesus). "**Death** (מָוֶת **Maveth**) **and life** (חַי **Khay or Chay**) **are in the power** (יָד **Yod or Yad**) **of the tongue** (לָשׁוֹן **Lashown**): and they that **love** (אָהַב **'Ahab**) it shall eat the **fruit** (פְּרִי **Periy**) thereof," is in reference to **the physical human tongue having the ability to positively or negatively put words into action**.

59

"And whatsoever we ask, we receive of him,
because we keep his commandments, and do those
things that are pleasing in his sight, KJV 1 John 3:22."

CHILDREN OF THE MOST HIGH:
PRISTINE YOUTH AND FAMILY SOLUTIONS, LLC.
SONS AND DAUGHTERS OF THE MOST HIGH PUBLISHERS

Oh, Gracious Most High Heavenly father, Holy is your name, Your Will Be Done Now and Forever!

In the KJV bible book of John chapter 1 verse 14; it states: "And **the Word was made flesh**, and dwelt among us, (and we beheld his glory, the glory as of the only begotten of the Father, full of grace and truth." The Messiah Yashu'a (Jesus) said: "I can of mine own self do nothing: as I hear, I judge: and my judgment is just; because I seek not mine own will, but the will of the Father which hath sent me, KJV John 5:30." "And we know that **all things work together for good to them that love God, to them who are the called according to** [his] **purpose**, KJV Romans 8:28." The Messiah Yashu'a (Jesus) said: "Ye have not chosen me, but I have chosen you, and ordained you, that ye should go and bring forth fruit, and [that] your fruit should remain: that whatsoever ye shall ask of the Father in my name, he may give it you, KJV John 15:16." **Words make up language, and words can be spoken or unspoken**.

60

"And whatsoever we ask, we receive of him, because we keep his commandments, and do those things that are pleasing in his sight, KJV 1 John 3:22."

Beware of the Pink Assassin (Your Tongue): The True Vine (Yashu'a, Jesus) Power of Life and Death is in the Tongue; Speaking God's (אלהים Elohîym) "Will" for Your Life into Existence!

CHILDREN OF THE MOST HIGH:
PRISTINE YOUTH AND FAMILY SOLUTIONS, LLC.
SONS AND DAUGHTERS OF THE MOST HIGH PUBLISHERS ®

Oh, Gracious Most High Heavenly father, Holy is your name, Your Will Be Done Now and Forever!

Therefore; like the Messiah Yashu'a (Jesus) said, <u>**the children of the Most High must continuously think the following words**</u>: "<u>On my own accord</u>, <u>I can of mine own self do nothing</u>, <u>I seek not mine own will, but the will of the Father which hath sent me</u>" according to the Most High Heavenly Father's pre<u>**ordained purpose**</u> for your life." <u>**The children of the Most High must continuously feel the following words**</u> **as treasures that we value in our hearts**: "<u>On my own accord</u>, <u>I can of mine own self do nothing</u>, <u>I seek not mine own will, but the will of the Father which hath sent me</u>" according to the Most High Heavenly Father's pre<u>**ordained purpose**</u> for your life."

61

"And whatsoever we ask, we receive of him, because we keep his commandments, and do those things that are pleasing in his sight, KJV 1 John 3:22."

Beware of the Pink Assassin (Your Tongue): The True Vine
(Yashu'a, Jesus) Power of Life and Death is in the Tongue;
Speaking God's (אלהים Eloĥîym) "Will"
for Your Life into Existence!

CHILDREN OF THE MOST HIGH:
PRISTINE YOUTH AND FAMILY SOLUTIONS, LLC.
SONS AND DAUGHTERS OF THE MOST HIGH PUBLISHERS ⚜

Oh, Gracious Most High Heavenly father, Holy is your name,
Your Will Be Done Now and Forever!

The children of the Most High must continuously **speak**

the following **words privately,** and **publicly** in

everyday conversations: "On my own accord, I can of mine

own self do nothing, I seek not mine own will, but the will of

the Father which hath sent me" according to the Most High

Heavenly Father's pre**ordained purpose** for your life."

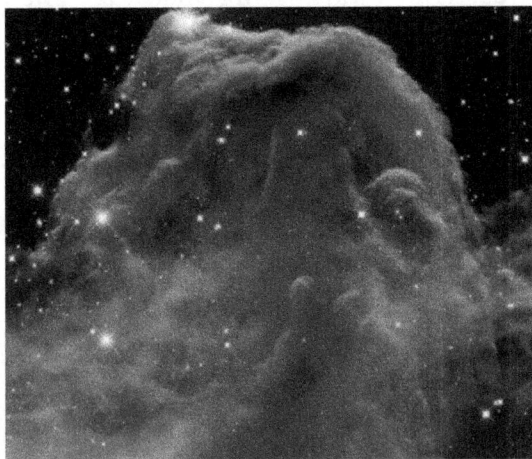

62

**"And whatsoever we ask, we receive of him,
because we keep his commandments, and do those
things that are pleasing in his sight, KJV 1 John 3:22."**

Beware of the Pink Assassin (Your Tongue): The True Vine
(Yashu'a, Jesus) Power of Life and Death is in the Tongue;
Speaking God's (אלהים Elohîym) "Will"
for Your Life into Existence!

CHILDREN OF THE MOST HIGH:
PRISTINE YOUTH AND FAMILY SOLUTIONS, LLC.
SONS AND DAUGHTERS OF THE MOST HIGH PUBLISHERS ®

Oh, Gracious Most High Heavenly father, Holy is your name,
Your Will Be Done Now and Forever!

The children of the Most High must continuously put the
following words in A.C.T.I.O.N. (Activated, Consciousness,
Timely, Intentions, Obligated, Now) through all of our
works, and in all that we are graciously blessed with the
opportunity to do: "On my own accord, I can of mine own
self do nothing, I seek not mine own will, but the will of the
Father which hath sent me" according to the Most High
Heavenly Father's pre**ordained** **purpose** for your life." **By**
thinking, saying, and doing the aforementioned; you can be
very successful at Mind Gardening in the Creative Garden
of Will (Your Mind) to grow the habit of speaking the True
Vine (Yashu'a, Jesus) Power of Life INTO EXISTENCE by
the "Will" of the Most High Heavenly Father for your life!

63

"And whatsoever we ask, we receive of him,
because we keep his commandments, and do those
things that are pleasing in his sight, KJV 1 John 3:22."

CHILDREN OF THE MOST HIGH:
PRISTINE YOUTH AND FAMILY SOLUTIONS, LLC.
SONS AND DAUGHTERS OF THE MOST HIGH PUBLISHERS ®

Oh, Gracious Most High Heavenly father, Holy is your name,
Your Will Be Done Now and Forever!

Chapter 2: You Can't Speak like Christ while you are still Thinking and Speaking like the Devil!

In the KJV bible book of Genesis chapter 11 verse 1-9; it states: "And the whole earth was of one **language** (שָׂפָה Saphah), and of one **speech** (דָּבָר Dabar). And it came to pass, as they journeyed from the east, that they found a plain in the land of Shinar; and they dwelt there. And they said one to another, Go to, let us make brick, and burn them throughly. And they had brick for stone, and slime had they for mortar. And they said, Go to, let us build us a city and a tower, whose top may reach unto heaven; and let us make us a name, lest we be scattered abroad upon the face of the whole earth. And the LORD came down to see the city and the tower, which the children of men built."

64

"And whatsoever we ask, we receive of him, because we keep his commandments, and do those things that are pleasing in his sight, KJV 1 John 3:22."

Beware of the Pink Assassin (Your Tongue): The True Vine
(Yashu'a, Jesus) Power of Life and Death is in the Tongue;
Speaking God's (אלהים Elohíym) "Will"
for Your Life into Existence!

CHILDREN OF THE MOST HIGH:
PRISTINE YOUTH AND FAMILY SOLUTIONS, LLC.
SONS AND DAUGHTERS OF THE MOST HIGH PUBLISHERS ®

Oh, Gracious Most High Heavenly father, Holy is your name,
Your Will Be Done Now and Forever!

"And the LORD said, Behold, the people are one, and they have
all one **language** (שָׂפָה Saphah); and this they begin to do: and
now nothing will be restrained from them, which they have
imagined to do. Go to, let us go down, and there **confound** (בָּלַל
Balal - to mix, mingle, confuse,) their **language** (שָׂפָה
Saphah), that they may not understand one another's **speech**
(דָּבָר Dabar). So, the LORD scattered them abroad from thence
upon the face of all the earth: and they left off to build the city.
Therefore, is the name of it called **Babel** (בָּבֶל Babel -
confusion); because the LORD did there **confound** (בָּלַל Balal)
the **language** (שָׂפָה Saphah) of all the earth: and from thence
did the LORD scatter them abroad upon the face of all the
earth." In the previous verses, the KJV bible Hebrew Strong's
Concordance "#8193 is שָׂפָה Saphah (pronounced as: **Saw-**
faw') for the word: "language." שָׂפָה Saphah is defined as:
language, lip, speech, talk words."

65

"And whatsoever we ask, we receive of him,
because we keep his commandments, and do those
things that are pleasing in his sight, KJV 1 John 3:22."

Beware of the Pink Assassin (Your Tongue): The True Vine (Yashu'a, Jesus) Power of Life and Death is in the Tongue; Speaking God's (אלהים Elohîym) "Will" for Your Life into Existence!

CHILDREN OF THE MOST HIGH:
PRISTINE YOUTH AND FAMILY SOLUTIONS, LLC.
SONS AND DAUGHTERS OF THE MOST HIGH PUBLISHERS ®

Oh, Gracious Most High Heavenly father, Holy is your name, Your Will Be Done Now and Forever!

The KJV bible Hebrew Strong's Concordance "**#1697** is דָּבָר **Dabar** (pronounced as: **Daw-baw'**) for the word: "**speech**." דָּבָר **Dabar** is defined as: speech, word, speaking, language, saying, utterance, word, words." The Online American Heritage Dictionary (2020), defines **language** as: "1. a. **Communication of thoughts and feelings through a system of arbitrary signals, such as voice sounds, gestures, or written symbols. b. Such a system including its rules for combining its components, such as words. c. Such a system as used by a nation, people, or other distinct community; often contrasted with dialect**. b. Computers A system of symbols and rules used for communication with or between computers. 3. **Body language; kinesics. Verbal communication as a subject of study**."

"And whatsoever we ask, we receive of him, because we keep his commandments, and do those things that are pleasing in his sight, KJV 1 John 3:22."

Beware of the Pink Assassin (Your Tongue): The True Vine (Yashu'a, Jesus) Power of Life and Death is in the Tongue; Speaking God's (אלהים Elohîym) "Will" for Your Life into Existence!

CHILDREN OF THE MOST HIGH:
PRISTINE YOUTH AND FAMILY SOLUTIONS, LLC.
SONS AND DAUGHTERS OF THE MOST HIGH PUBLISHERS ®

Oh, Gracious Most High Heavenly father, Holy is your name, Your Will Be Done Now and Forever!

"**Word** is defined as: **A sound or a combination of sounds, or its representation in writing or printing, that symbolizes and communicates a meaning**. **Something said; an utterance, remark, or comment**: b. **A command or direction; an order**: gave the word to retreat. c. **An assurance or promise**; sworn intention; d. **A verbal signal; a password or watchword**. a. **Discourse or talk; speech**: Actions speak louder than words. b. **In music, the text of a vocal composition; lyrics. Word**: a. **See Logos**. b. **The Scriptures; the Bible**. **Speech** is defined as: **The faculty or act of speaking**. b. **The faculty or act of expressing or describing thoughts, feelings, or perceptions by the articulation of words**. 2. a. **What is spoken or expressed, as in conversation; uttered or written words**: A talk or public address, or a written copy of this."

"And whatsoever we ask, we receive of him, because we keep his commandments, and do those things that are pleasing in his sight, KJV 1 John 3:22."

Beware of the Pink Assassin (Your Tongue): The True Vine
(Yashu'a, Jesus) Power of Life and Death is in the Tongue;
Speaking God's (אלהים Elŏhîym) "Will"
for Your Life into Existence!

CHILDREN OF THE MOST HIGH:
PRISTINE YOUTH AND FAMILY SOLUTIONS, LLC.
SONS AND DAUGHTERS OF THE MOST HIGH PUBLISHERS

*Oh, Gracious Most High Heavenly father, Holy is your name,
Your Will Be Done Now and Forever!*

"3.a. **The language or dialect of a nation or region**: b. **One's manner or style of speaking**: 4. **The study of oral communication, speech sounds, and vocal physiology**. Tongue is defined as: a. **The fleshy, movable, muscular organ, attached in most vertebrates to the floor of the mouth, that is the principal organ of taste, an aid in chewing and swallowing, and, in humans, an important organ of speech**." The KJV bible Hebrew Strong's Concordance "# 3956 is לָשׁוֹן **Lashown** for the word: "**tongue**" (pronounced as: Law-shone). לָשׁוֹן **Lashown** is defined as: **the tongue of a person** or animals, **used literally as the instrument of** licking, eating, or **speech**), **and figuratively** (**speech**, an ingot, a fork of flame, a cove of water): babbler, bay, evil speaker, language, talker, wedge."

68

**"And whatsoever we ask, we receive of him,
because we keep his commandments, and do those
things that are pleasing in his sight, KJV 1 John 3:22."**

Beware of the Pink Assassin (Your Tongue): The True Vine (Yashu'a, Jesus) Power of Life and Death is in the Tongue;
Speaking God's (אלהים Elŏhîym) "Will" for Your Life into Existence!

CHILDREN OF THE MOST HIGH:
PRISTINE YOUTH AND FAMILY SOLUTIONS, LLC.
SONS AND DAUGHTERS OF THE MOST HIGH PUBLISHERS ℗

Oh, Gracious Most High Heavenly father, Holy is your name,
Your Will Be Done Now and Forever!

The KJV bible Greek Strong's Concordance **"#1100** is γλῶσσα **Glōssa** for the word: **"tongue"** (pronounced as: **Gloce-sah'**). γλῶσσα **Glōssa** is defined as: **the tongue, a member of the body, an organ of speech, a tongue - the language or dialect used by a particular people distinct from that of other nations**." So, according to the Mayo Clinic (2020), "Speech occurs when air flows from the lungs, up the windpipe (trachea) and through the voice box (larynx). This causes the vocal cords to vibrate, creating sound. Sound is shaped into words by the muscles controlling the soft palate, tongue and lips."

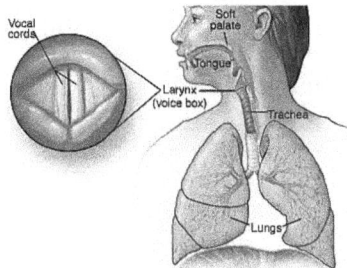

69

"And whatsoever we ask, we receive of him, because we keep his commandments, and do those things that are pleasing in his sight, KJV 1 John 3:22."

Beware of the Pink Assassin (Your Tongue): The True Vine
(Yashu'a, Jesus) Power of Life and Death is in the Tongue;
Speaking God's (אלהים Elohîym) "Will"
for Your Life into Existence!

CHILDREN OF THE MOST HIGH:
PRISTINE YOUTH AND FAMILY SOLUTIONS, LLC.
SONS AND DAUGHTERS OF THE MOST HIGH PUBLISHERS ®

*Oh, Gracious Most High Heavenly father, Holy is your name,
Your Will Be Done Now and Forever!*

Who are the Pharisees? And what did the Messiah Yashu'a (Jesus) say about speaking words, and knowing the thoughts of the Pharisees in the KJV bible book of Mathews chapter 12 verses 24-37?

According the KJV bible Greek Strong's Concordance "#5330 Φαρισαῖος Pharisaios for the word: "Pharisees." The Φαρισαῖος Pharisaios were: "A sect that seems to have started after the Jewish exile. In addition to OT books the Pharisees recognized in oral tradition a standard of belief and life. They sought for distinction and praise by outward observance of external rites and by outward forms of piety, and such as ceremonial washings, fasting, prayers, and alms giving; and, comparatively negligent of genuine piety, they prided themselves on their fancied good works."

**"And whatsoever we ask, we receive of him,
because we keep his commandments, and do those
things that are pleasing in his sight, KJV 1 John 3:22."**

Beware of the Pink Assassin (Your Tongue): The True Vine
(Yashu'a, Jesus) Power of Life and Death is in the Tongue;
Speaking God's (אלהים Elóhîym) "Will"
for Your Life into Existence!

CHILDREN OF THE MOST HIGH:
PRISTINE YOUTH AND FAMILY SOLUTIONS, LLC.
SONS AND DAUGHTERS OF THE MOST HIGH PUBLISHERS ®

*Oh, Gracious Most High Heavenly father, Holy is your name,
Your Will Be Done Now and Forever!*

"They held strenuously to a belief in the existence of good and
evil angels, and to the expectation of a Messiah; and they
cherished the hope that the dead, after a preliminary experience
either of reward or of penalty in Hades, would be recalled to life
by him, and be requited each according to his individual deeds.
In opposition to the usurped dominion of the Herod's and the
rule of the Romans, **they stoutly upheld the theocracy and
their country's cause, and possessed great influence with the
common people**. According to Josephus they numbered more
than 6000. **They were bitter enemies of Yashu'a (Jesus) and
his cause; and were in turn severely rebuked by him for
their avarice, ambition, hollow reliance on outward works,
and affection of piety in order to gain popularity**."

71
**"And whatsoever we ask, we receive of him,
because we keep his commandments, and do those
things that are pleasing in his sight, KJV 1 John 3:22."**

Beware of the Pink Assassin (Your Tongue): The True Vine (Yashu'a, Jesus) Power of Life and Death is in the Tongue; **Speaking God's (אלהים Elohîym) "Will" for Your Life into Existence!**

Oh, Gracious Most High Heavenly father, Holy is your name, Your Will Be Done Now and Forever!

In the KJV bible book of Mathews chapter 12 verses 24-37; it states: "But when the Pharisees heard it, they said, this fellow doth not cast out devils, but by Beelzebub the prince of the devils. **And Jesus knew their thoughts**, and said unto them; "Every kingdom divided against itself is brought to desolation; and every city or house divided against itself shall not stand. And if Satan cast out Satan, he is divided against himself; how shall then his kingdom stand? And if I by Beelzebub cast out devils, by whom do your children cast them out? therefore they shall be your judges. But if I cast out devils by the Spirit of God, then the kingdom of God is come unto you. Or else how can one enter into a strong man's house, and spoil his goods, except he first bind the strong man? and then he will spoil his house."

"And whatsoever we ask, we receive of him, because we keep his commandments, and do those things that are pleasing in his sight, KJV 1 John 3:22."

Beware of the Pink Assassin (Your Tongue): The True Vine (Yashu'a, Jesus) Power of Life and Death is in the Tongue; Speaking God's (אלהים Elohîym) "Will" for Your Life into Existence!

CHILDREN OF THE MOST HIGH:
PRISTINE YOUTH AND FAMILY SOLUTIONS, LLC.
SONS AND DAUGHTERS OF THE MOST HIGH PUBLISHERS ®

Oh, Gracious Most High Heavenly father, Holy is your name, Your Will Be Done Now and Forever!

"He that is not with me is against me; and he that gathered not with me scattereth abroad. Wherefore I say unto you, all manner of sin and blasphemy shall be forgiven unto men: but the blasphemy against the Holy Ghost shall not be forgiven unto men. And whosoever speaketh a word against the Son of man, it shall be forgiven him: but whosoever speaketh against the Holy Ghost, it shall not be forgiven him, neither in this world, neither in the world to come. Either make the tree good, and his fruit good; or else make the tree corrupt, and his fruit corrupt: for the tree is known by his fruit. O generation of vipers, how can ye, being evil, speak good things? for out of the abundance of the heart the mouth speaketh. A good man (ἄνθρωπος Anthrōpos – person, human being) out of the good treasure of the heart bringeth forth good things: and an evil man out of the evil treasure bringeth forth evil things."

73

"And whatsoever we ask, we receive of him, because we keep his commandments, and do those things that are pleasing in his sight, KJV 1 John 3:22."

Beware of the Pink Assassin (Your Tongue): The True Vine
(Yashu'a, Jesus) Power of Life and Death is in the Tongue;
Speaking God's (אלהים Elŏhîym) "Will"
for Your Life into Existence!

CHILDREN OF THE MOST HIGH:
PRISTINE YOUTH AND FAMILY SOLUTIONS, LLC.
SONS AND DAUGHTERS OF THE MOST HIGH PUBLISHERS ®

Oh, Gracious Most High Heavenly father, Holy is your name,
Your Will Be Done Now and Forever!

"But I say unto you, that every idle (ἀργός Argos - (as a
negative particle) inactive, (by implication) lazy, useless:
barren, idle, slow) word that men (ἄνθρωπος Anthrōpos –
people, human beings) shall speak, they shall give account
thereof in the day of judgment. For by thy words thou shalt
be justified, and by thy words thou shalt be condemned."

According to the aforementioned verses, spoken words are a
reflection of how a person thinks in their mind, and a reflection
of how they feel in their heart. So, Yashu'a (Jesus) said: A good
man (ἄνθρωπος Anthrōpos – person, human being) out of
the good treasure of the heart bringeth forth good things:
and an evil man out of the evil treasure bringeth forth evil
things."

74
"And whatsoever we ask, we receive of him,
because we keep his commandments, and do those
things that are pleasing in his sight, KJV 1 John 3:22."

Beware of the Pink Assassin (Your Tongue): The True Vine (Yashu'a, Jesus) Power of Life and Death is in the Tongue; Speaking God's (אלהים Elohîym) "Will" for Your Life into Existence!

CHILDREN OF THE MOST HIGH: PRISTINE YOUTH AND FAMILY SOLUTIONS, LLC. SONS AND DAUGHTERS OF THE MOST HIGH PUBLISHERS ®

Oh, Gracious Most High Heavenly father, Holy is your name, Your Will Be Done Now and Forever!

Therefore, **a person can't speak like Christ while still Thinking and Speaking like the Devil!** <u>**The children of the Most High must continuously put the following words in A.C.T.I.O.N. (Activated, Consciousness, Timely, Intentions, Obligated, Now) through all of our works, and in all that we are graciously blessed with the opportunity to do**</u>: "<u>On my own accord</u>, <u>I can of mine own self do nothing</u>, <u>I seek not mine own will, but the will of the Father which hath sent me</u>" according to the Most High Heavenly Father's pre<u>**ordained purpose**</u> for your life." <u>**By thinking, saying, and doing the aforementioned; you can be very successful at**</u> Mind Gardening in the Creative Garden of Will (Your Mind) to grow the habit of speaking the True Vine (Yashu'a, Jesus) Power of Life INTO EXISTENCE by the "Will" of the Most High Heavenly Father <u>for your life</u>!

75

"And whatsoever we ask, we receive of him, because we keep his commandments, and do those things that are pleasing in his sight, KJV 1 John 3:22."

Beware of the Pink Assassin (Your Tongue): The True Vine
(Yashu'a, Jesus) Power of Life and Death is in the Tongue;
Speaking God's (אלהים Elŏhîym) "Will"
for Your Life into Existence!

CHILDREN OF THE MOST HIGH:
PRISTINE YOUTH AND FAMILY SOLUTIONS, LLC.
SONS AND DAUGHTERS OF THE MOST HIGH PUBLISHERS ®

Oh, Gracious Most High Heavenly father, Holy is your name,
Your Will Be Done Now and Forever!

Chapter 3: Are there Hateful Words that are rooted in the foundation of the 9 Deadly Venoms of the Desires of the great dragon, that old serpent, called the devil and satan that deceived the whole world (KJV Revelation 12:7-9)?

In the KJV bible book of Titus chapter 3 verse 3; it states: "For we ourselves also were sometimes **foolish, disobedient, deceived, serving divers lusts and pleasures, living in malice and envy, <u>hateful</u>, and hating one another**." According to the KJV bible Greek Strong's Concordance "**#4767 στυγητός Stygētos (pronounced as: Stoog-nay-tos')** is the word for: "<u>hateful</u>." στυγητός Stygētos is defined as: (**to hate**); **hated, detestable, odious**: —hateful." The Online American Heritage Dictionary (2020) defines **hateful** as: "**Eliciting or deserving hatred. 2. Feeling or showing hatred**: 3. **Informal Very unpleasant or unappealing**."

76

"And whatsoever we ask, we receive of him, because we keep his commandments, and do those things that are pleasing in his sight, KJV 1 John 3:22."

Beware of the Pink Assassin (Your Tongue): The True Vine (Yashu'a, Jesus) Power of Life and Death is in the Tongue; Speaking God's (אלהים Elohîym) "Will" for Your Life into Existence!

CHILDREN OF THE MOST HIGH:
PRISTINE YOUTH AND FAMILY SOLUTIONS, LLC.
SONS AND DAUGHTERS OF THE MOST HIGH PUBLISHERS ®

Oh, Gracious Most High Heavenly father, Holy is your name, Your Will Be Done Now and Forever!

In the KJV bible book of Revelation chapter 12 verse 12; it states: "Therefore rejoice, ye heavens, and ye that dwell in them. <u>Woe to the inhibiters of the earth and of the sea</u>! <u>for the devil is come down unto you, having great wrath, because he knoweth that he hath but a short time</u>."

Did the devil bring messages of hate and hateful words to the planet earth?

In the KJV bible book of **Revelation** chapter **12** verses **7-9**; it states: "And there was war in heaven: <u>**Michael and his angels**</u> (ἄγγελος **Angelos, meaning Messengers** according to <u>the KJV bible Greek Strong's Concordance #32</u>) fought against the **dragon**; and <u>**the dragon fought and his angels**</u> (ἄγγελος **Angelos, meaning Messengers**, and prevailed not; neither was their place found any more in heaven."

77

"And whatsoever we ask, we receive of him, because we keep his commandments, and do those things that are pleasing in his sight, KJV 1 John 3:22."

Beware of the Pink Assassin (Your Tongue): The True Vine (Yashu'a, Jesus) Power of Life and Death is in the Tongue; Speaking God's (אלהים Elôhîym) "Will" for Your Life into Existence!

CHILDREN OF THE MOST HIGH:
PRISTINE YOUTH AND FAMILY SOLUTIONS, LLC.
SONS AND DAUGHTERS OF THE MOST HIGH PUBLISHERS ®

Oh, Gracious Most High Heavenly father, Holy is your name, Your Will Be Done Now and Forever!

"And the **great dragon** was cast out, that **old serpent**, **called the Devil, and Satan**, which deceiveth the whole world: he was cast out into the earth, and his **angels** (ἄγγελος **Angelos**, **meaning Messengers**, were cast out with him." **Since angels are messengers, how does messages of the great dragon: that old serpent, called the Devil, and Satan, which deceiveth the whole world and his angels** and the **messages of Michael and his angels** relate to all members of humanity?

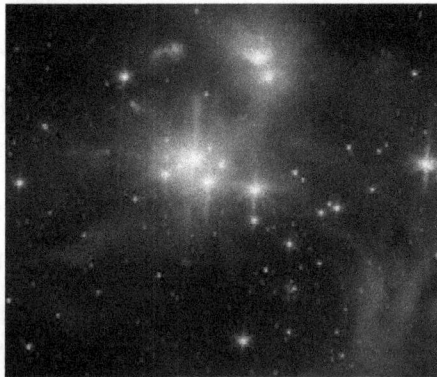

78

"And whatsoever we ask, we receive of him, because we keep his commandments, and do those things that are pleasing in his sight, KJV 1 John 3:22."

Beware of the Pink Assassin (Your Tongue): The True Vine (Yashu'a, Jesus) Power of Life and Death is in the Tongue; Speaking God's (אלהים Elohîym) "Will" for Your Life into Existence!

CHILDREN OF THE MOST HIGH:
PRISTINE YOUTH AND FAMILY SOLUTIONS, LLC.
SONS AND DAUGHTERS OF THE MOST HIGH PUBLISHERS ®

Oh, Gracious Most High Heavenly father, Holy is your name, Your Will Be Done Now and Forever!

The great dragon: that old serpent, called the Devil, and Satan, which deceiveth the whole world and his angels (ἄγγελος **Angelos, meaning Messengers**), spread **messages** of the **9 Deadly Venoms of the Desires of the great dragon: that old serpent, called the Devil, and Satan**, which according to the Children of the Most High: Pristine Youth and Family Solutions, LLC., are: **Slothful**, **Wrath**, **Pride**, **Greed**, **Lust**, **Hopeless Fear Disobedience**, **Lying**, **Heinous Murde**r, and **Wickedness**. **Additional devil messages of hate and hateful words that were brought to the planet earth** by the devil and his angels are shown on the Children of the Most High: Pristine Youth and Family Solutions, LLC., Devil's Web Logo on the next page.

79

"And whatsoever we ask, we receive of him, because we keep his commandments, and do those things that are pleasing in his sight, KJV 1 John 3:22."

Beware of the Pink Assassin (Your Tongue): The True Vine
(Yashu'a, Jesus) Power of Life and Death is in the Tongue;
Speaking God's (אלהים Elohîym) "Will"
for Your Life into Existence!

CHILDREN OF THE MOST HIGH:
PRISTINE YOUTH AND FAMILY SOLUTIONS, LLC.
SONS AND DAUGHTERS OF THE MOST HIGH PUBLISHERS ®

*Oh, Gracious Most High Heavenly father, Holy is your name,
Your Will Be Done Now and Forever!*

CHILDREN OF THE MOST HIGH:
PRISTINE YOUTH AND FAMILY SOLUTIONS, LLC.
SONS AND DAUGHTERS OF THE MOST HIGH PUBLISHERS ®

THE DEVIL'S WEB

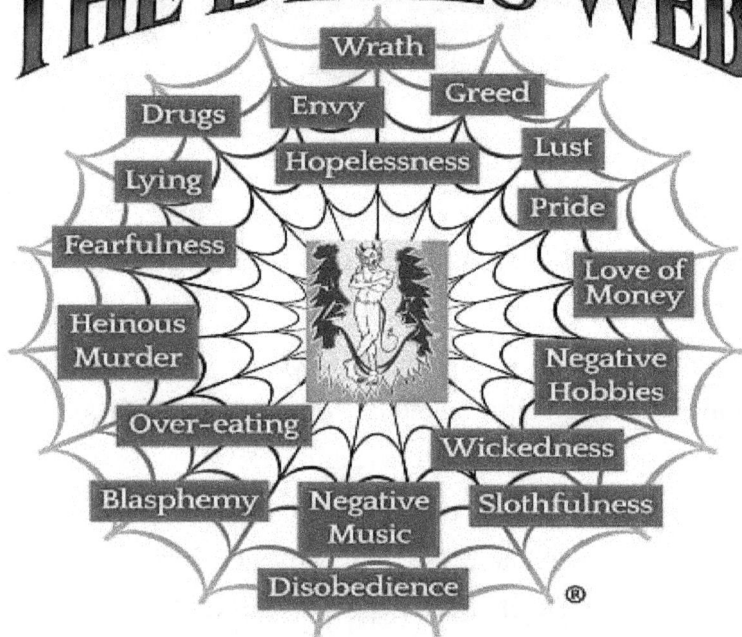

Wrath
Envy
Greed
Drugs
Hopelessness
Lust
Lying
Pride
Fearfulness
Love of Money
Heinous Murder
Negative Hobbies
Over-eating
Wickedness
Blasphemy
Negative Music
Slothfulness
Disobedience
®

80

**"And whatsoever we ask, we receive of him,
because we keep his commandments, and do those
things that are pleasing in his sight, KJV 1 John 3:22."**

Beware of the Pink Assassin (Your Tongue): The True Vine (Yashu'a, Jesus) Power of Life and Death is in the Tongue; Speaking God's (אלהים Elóhîym) "Will" for Your Life into Existence!

CHILDREN OF THE MOST HIGH:
PRISTINE YOUTH AND FAMILY SOLUTIONS, LLC.
SONS AND DAUGHTERS OF THE MOST HIGH PUBLISHERS ®

Oh, Gracious Most High Heavenly father, Holy is your name, Your Will Be Done Now and Forever!

Some of the messages of **Michael and his angels** (ἄγγελος **Angelos)** are in the KJV bible book of Hebrews chapter 8 verses 10-16; states: **"For this is the covenant that I will make with the house of Israel after those days, saith the Lord; I will put my laws into their mind, and write them in their hearts: and I will be to them a God, and they shall be to me a people. And they shall not teach every man his neighbour, and every man his brother, saying, Know the Lord: for all shall know me, from the least to the greatest. For I will be merciful to their unrighteousness, and their sins and their iniquities will I remember no more. In that he saith, a new covenant, he hath made the first old. Now that which decayeth and waxeth old is ready to vanish away."**

81

"And whatsoever we ask, we receive of him, because we keep his commandments, and do those things that are pleasing in his sight, KJV 1 John 3:22."

Beware of the Pink Assassin (Your Tongue): The True Vine (Yashu'a, Jesus) Power of Life and Death is in the Tongue; **Speaking God's (אלהים א Elohíym) "Will" for Your Life into Existence!**

Oh, Gracious Most High Heavenly father, Holy is your name, Your Will Be Done Now and Forever!

"**Whereof the Holy Ghost also is a witness to us: for after that he had said before, this is the covenant that I will make with them after those days, saith the Lord, I will put my laws into their hearts, and in their minds will I write them.**" In the KJV bible book of Revelation chapter 22 verses 14-16; Yashu'a (Jesus) saith "Blessed are they that do his commandments, that they may have right to the tree of life, and may enter in through the gates into the city." In the KJV bible book of John chapter 14 verse 6; Yashu'a (Jesus) saith unto him, "I am the way, the truth, and the life: no man cometh unto the Father, but by me." In the KJV bible book of Matthew chapter 22 verses 37-38; Yashu'a (Jesus) said unto him: "Thou shalt love the Lord thy God with all thy heart, and with all thy soul, and with all thy mind. This is the first and great commandment."

"And whatsoever we ask, we receive of him, because we keep his commandments, and do those things that are pleasing in his sight, KJV 1 John 3:22."

Beware of the Pink Assassin (Your Tongue): The True Vine (Yashu'a, Jesus) Power of Life and Death is in the Tongue; Speaking God's (אלהים Elohîym) "Will" for Your Life into Existence!

CHILDREN OF THE MOST HIGH:
PRISTINE YOUTH AND FAMILY SOLUTIONS, LLC.
SONS AND DAUGHTERS OF THE MOST HIGH PUBLISHERS ®

Oh, Gracious Most High Heavenly father, Holy is your name, Your Will Be Done Now and Forever!

Therefore, each person on the planet earth is either a knowing or unknowing advocate of the **messages of the great dragon, that old serpent called the devil and satan** which deceiveth the whole world **or an advocate of the messages of the Arch Angelic-Being Miykaa'iyl (Micha-El-means who dares to be like the Most High (ELYOWN עֶלְיוֹן EL אֵל)** by the purpose of why and how they live their lives, the way they think, <u>the words they speak</u>, their actions and deeds.

> Watch your *thoughts;*
> they become words.
> Watch your *words;* they
> become actions.
> Watch your *actions;* they
> become habits.
> Watch your *habits;* they
> become character.
> Watch your *character;* it
> becomes your *destiny.*
> -Lao-Tze

83

"And whatsoever we ask, we receive of him, because we keep his commandments, and do those things that are pleasing in his sight, KJV 1 John 3:22."

Beware of the Pink Assassin (Your Tongue): The True Vine (Yashu'a, Jesus) Power of Life and Death is in the Tongue; Speaking God's (אלהים Elŏhîym) "Will" for Your Life into Existence!

CHILDREN OF THE MOST HIGH:
PRISTINE YOUTH AND FAMILY SOLUTIONS, LLC.
SONS AND DAUGHTERS OF THE MOST HIGH PUBLISHERS ®

Oh, Gracious Most High Heavenly father, Holy is your name, Your Will Be Done Now and Forever!

So, the previous bible verses reveal that there are **Hateful Words** that are **rooted in the foundation** of the **9 Deadly Venoms of the Desires of the great dragon, that old serpent, called the devil and satan that deceived the whole world!** Therefore; in an effort to not utilize hateful words; **the children of the Most High must continuously put the following words in A.C.T.I.O.N. (Activated, Consciousness, Timely, Intentions, Obligated, Now) through all of our works, and in all that we are graciously blessed with the opportunity to do**: "On my own accord, I can of mine own self do nothing, I seek not mine own will, but the will of the Father which hath sent me" according to the Most High Heavenly Father's pre**ordained** **purpose** for your life." **By thinking, saying, and doing the aforementioned; you can be very successful at Mind Gardening in the Creative Garden of Will (Your Mind) to grow the habit of speaking the True Vine (Yashu'a, Jesus) Power of Life INTO EXISTENCE by the "Will" of the Most High Heavenly Father for your life!**

84

"And whatsoever we ask, we receive of him, because we keep his commandments, and do those things that are pleasing in his sight, KJV 1 John 3:22."

CHILDREN OF THE MOST HIGH:
PRISTINE YOUTH AND FAMILY SOLUTIONS, LLC.
SONS AND DAUGHTERS OF THE MOST HIGH PUBLISHERS ®

Oh, Gracious Most High Heavenly father, Holy is your name, Your Will Be Done Now and Forever!

Chapter 4: Are there Love Words that are rooted in the Foundation of the True Vine (Yashu'a, Jesus) Fruits of the Spirit of Positive Character-Building Essentials?

85

"And whatsoever we ask, we receive of him, because we keep his commandments, and do those things that are pleasing in his sight, KJV 1 John 3:22."

Oh, Gracious Most High Heavenly father, Holy is your name, Your Will Be Done Now and Forever!

Are there Love Words that are rooted in the Foundation of the True Vine (Yashu'a, Jesus) Fruits of the Spirit of Positive Character-Building Essentials?

Yes! According to the KJV bible book of Galatians chapter 5 verses 22-23; it states: "But the **fruit of the Spirit is <u>love</u>, <u>joy</u>, <u>peace</u>, <u>longsuffering</u>, <u>gentleness</u>, <u>goodness</u>, <u>faith</u>, <u>Meekness</u>, <u>temperance</u>**: against such there is no law." The Children of the Most High: Pristine Youth and Family Solutions, LLC., refer to the aforementioned fruits as: <u>**Love Words that are rooted in the Foundation of the True Vine (Yashu'a, Jesus) Fruits of the Spirit of Positive Character-Building Essentials. The 9 True Vine (Yashu'a, Jesus) Fruits of the Spirit of Positive Character-Building Essentials**</u> are:

"And whatsoever we ask, we receive of him, because we keep his commandments, and do those things that are pleasing in his sight, KJV 1 John 3:22."

CHILDREN OF THE MOST HIGH:
PRISTINE YOUTH AND FAMILY SOLUTIONS, LLC.
SONS AND DAUGHTERS OF THE MOST HIGH PUBLISHERS ®

Oh, Gracious Most High Heavenly father, Holy is your name,
Your Will Be Done Now and Forever!

1: "**Love** – ἀγάπη Agápē, Ag-ah'-pay; from KJV Bible Greek Strong's Concordance **#25**; which means: **love**, i.e. affection or benevolence; specially (plural) a love-feast: — (feast of) charity(-ably), dear, love. Affection, good will, love, benevolence, brotherly love, love feasts. In KJV bible book of Galatians chapter 5 verse 22; it states: "But the fruit of the Spirit is **love**, joy, peace, longsuffering, gentleness, goodness, faith."

87

"And whatsoever we ask, we receive of him, because we keep his commandments, and do those things that are pleasing in his sight, KJV 1 John 3:22."

Beware of the Pink Assassin (Your Tongue): The True Vine
(Yashu'a, Jesus) Power of Life and Death is in the Tongue;
Speaking God's (אלהים Elơhîym) "Will"
for Your Life into Existence!

*Oh, Gracious Most High Heavenly father, Holy is your name,
Your Will Be Done Now and Forever!*

The True Vine Yashu'a (Jesus) Fruit of the Spirit of
Positive Character-Building Essential of "<u>Love</u>" through
true-faith in the Most High Heavenly Father is used to
overcome and resist the 5th of the 9 Deadly Venoms of the
Desires of the great dragon, that old serpent called the devil
and satan which deceiveth the whole world known as "**Lust**"
by expressing divine love for the Most High Heavenly Father,
loving the Messiah Yashu'a to overcoming the longing for
something that is forbidden (**Love – ἀγάπη Agápē**) according
to the commandments of the Most High.

88

**"And whatsoever we ask, we receive of him,
because we keep his commandments, and do those
things that are pleasing in his sight, KJV 1 John 3:22."**

Beware of the Pink Assassin (Your Tongue): The True Vine (Yashu'a, Jesus) Power of Life and Death is in the Tongue; Speaking God's (אלהים Elốhíym) "Will" for Your Life into Existence!

CHILDREN OF THE MOST HIGH:
PRISTINE YOUTH AND FAMILY SOLUTIONS, LLC.
SONS AND DAUGHTERS OF THE MOST HIGH PUBLISHERS ®

Oh, Gracious Most High Heavenly father, Holy is your name, Your Will Be Done Now and Forever!

2: "**Joy** – χαρά **Chará, Khar-ah'**; from KJV Bible Greek Strong's Concordance #**5463**; which means: **cheerfulness**, i.e. calm delight:—gladness, × greatly, (X be exceeding) joy(-ful, -ully, -fulness, -ous). Joy, gladness, the joy received from you, the cause or occasion of joy, of persons who are one's joy. In KJV bible book of Galatians chapter 5 verse 22; it states: "But the fruit of the Spirit is love, **joy**, peace, longsuffering, gentleness, goodness, faith." According to "**The will to Kill**": **Making sense of senseless murder** (2018), over 90% of all **Heinous Murder**s were committed by people who were not joyful, but were very angry or enraged. The **True Vine Yashu'a (Jesus) Fruit of the Spirit of Positive Character-Building Essential of "Joy"** through true-faith in the Most High Heavenly Father is used to overcome and resist the **8th of the 9 Deadly Venoms of the Desires of the great dragon, that old serpent called the devil and satan which deceiveth the whole world** known as "**Heinous Murder**" by learning and practicing being happy inside, **cheerful, calm** and **delightful** (**Joy** – χαρά **Chará, Khar-ah'**) every day."

89

"And whatsoever we ask, we receive of him, because we keep his commandments, and do those things that are pleasing in his sight, KJV 1 John 3:22."

Beware of the Pink Assassin (Your Tongue): The True Vine
(Yashu'a, Jesus) Power of Life and Death is in the Tongue;
Speaking God's (אלהים Elŏhîym) "Will"
for Your Life into Existence!

CHILDREN OF THE MOST HIGH:
PRISTINE YOUTH AND FAMILY SOLUTIONS, LLC.
SONS AND DAUGHTERS OF THE MOST HIGH PUBLISHERS ®

*Oh, Gracious Most High Heavenly father, Holy is your name,
Your Will Be Done Now and Forever!*

3: "<u>Peace</u> – εἰρήνη **Eirénē**, **i-ray'-nay**; from KJV Bible Greek
Strong's Concordance "**#1515** probably from a primary verb εἴρω
eírō (to join); which means: **peace** (literally or figuratively); by
implication, prosperity: one, peace, quietness, rest, + set at one
again. A state of national tranquility, exemption from the rage and
havoc of war, peace between individuals, i.e., harmony, concord,
security, safety, prosperity, felicity, (because peace and harmony
make and keep things safe and prosperous); of the Messiah's
peace, the way that leads to peace (salvation), the blessed state of
devout and upright men after death. In KJV bible book of
Galatians chapter 5 verse 22; it states: "But the fruit of the Spirit
is love, joy, **peace**, longsuffering, gentleness, goodness, faith."
The **True Vine Yashu'a (Jesus) Fruit of the Spirit of Positive
Character-Building Essential of** "Peace" through true-faith in
the Most High Heavenly Father is used to overcome and resist the
**7th of the 9 Deadly Venoms of the Desires of the great dragon,
that old serpent called the devil and satan which deceiveth the
whole world** known as "Lying" by learning and practicing being
peaceful, devout and upright (Peace – εἰρήνη Eirénē)."

90

**"And whatsoever we ask, we receive of him,
because we keep his commandments, and do those
things that are pleasing in his sight, KJV 1 John 3:22."**

Beware of the Pink Assassin (Your Tongue): The True Vine
(Yashu'a, Jesus) Power of Life and Death is in the Tongue;
Speaking God's (אלהים Elôhîym) "Will"
for Your Life into Existence!

CHILDREN OF THE MOST HIGH:
PRISTINE YOUTH AND FAMILY SOLUTIONS, LLC.
SONS AND DAUGHTERS OF THE MOST HIGH PUBLISHERS ®

*Oh, Gracious Most High Heavenly father, Holy is your name,
Your Will Be Done Now and Forever!*

4: "**Longsuffering** – μακροθυμία **makrothymía**, mak-roth-
oo-mee'-ah; longanimity, i.e. which means: (objectively)
forbearance or (subjectively) fortitude, **patience**, endurance,
constancy, steadfastness, perseverance, longsuffering, slowness
in avenging wrongs. In KJV bible book of Galatians chapter 5
verse 22; it states: "But the fruit of the Spirit is love, joy, peace,
longsuffering, gentleness, goodness, faith." The **True Vine
Yashu'a (Jesus) Fruit of the Spirit of Positive Character-
Building Essential** of "longsuffering" through true-faith in the
Most High Heavenly Father is used to overcome and resist the
**2nd of the 9 Deadly Venoms of the Desires of the great
dragon, that old serpent called the devil and satan which
deceiveth the whole world** known as "**Wrath**" by learning and
practicing **longsuffering μακροθυμία makrothymía** which
overcomes   **Wrath**." Wrath is a negative unhealthy energy in
action through e-motion or energy in motion ($E=mc^2$). When a
person gives into wrath, for those moments, they are literally
out of their positive mind and are controlled by emotions.
Energy in motion equals emotions ($E=mc^2$) which can become
dangerous when they are in motion. These are the identical
emotions that are the roots for hate, war, lust, greed, envy, pride
and fear.

91

**"And whatsoever we ask, we receive of him,
because we keep his commandments, and do those
things that are pleasing in his sight, KJV 1 John 3:22."**

Beware of the Pink Assassin (Your Tongue): The True Vine
(Yashu'a, Jesus) Power of Life and Death is in the Tongue;
Speaking God's (אלהים Elóhîym) "Will"
for Your Life into Existence!

CHILDREN OF THE MOST HIGH:
PRISTINE YOUTH AND FAMILY SOLUTIONS, LLC.
SONS AND DAUGHTERS OF THE MOST HIGH PUBLISHERS ®

*Oh, Gracious Most High Heavenly father, Holy is your name,
Your Will Be Done Now and Forever!*

5: "**Gentleness** – **Chrēstotēs** χρηστότης KJV Bible Greek
Strong's Concordance **#5544** which means: **khray-stot'-ace**; from
usefulness, i.e., **morally**, **excellence** (in character or demeanor):
—gentleness, **good(-ness), kindness**. Overcomes being **Slothful**.
In KJV bible book of Galatians chapter 5 verse 22; it states: "But
the fruit of the Spirit is love, joy, peace, longsuffering, **gentleness**,
goodness, faith." So, a person who has **accepted the Lord Jesus
Christ (Yashu'a Ha Mashiakh – Jesus the Messiah or
Yehoshu'a – Yahayyu is Salvation or Yahayyu Saves) as their
Savior, is in the Body of Christ** and can access **the True Vine
Yashu'a (Jesus) Fruits of the Spirit Positive Character-
Building Essentials** of "**Gentleness** – Chrēstotēs (χρηστότης)"
through true-faith in the Most High Heavenly Father is used to
overcome and resist the **1 of 9 Deadly Venoms of the Desires of
the great dragon, that old serpent called the devil and satan
which deceiveth the whole world** known as "**Slothfulness**" by
being kind to all life and positively useful every day.

92

**"And whatsoever we ask, we receive of him,
because we keep his commandments, and do those
things that are pleasing in his sight, KJV 1 John 3:22."**

CHILDREN OF THE MOST HIGH:
PRISTINE YOUTH AND FAMILY SOLUTIONS, LLC.
SONS AND DAUGHTERS OF THE MOST HIGH PUBLISHERS ®

Oh, Gracious Most High Heavenly father, Holy is your name,
Your Will Be Done Now and Forever!

6: "<u>Goodness</u> - ἀγαθωσύνη Agathōsýnē, ag-ath-o-soo'-nay; from KJV Bible Greek Strong's Concordance **#18**; which means: **goodness**, **uprightness of heart and life**, **kindness**, i.e. virtue or beneficence. In KJV bible book of Galatians chapter 5 verse 22; it states: "But the fruit of the Spirit is love, joy, peace, longsuffering, gentleness, **goodness**, faith." The **True Vine Yashu'a (Jesus) Fruit of the Spirit of Positive Character-Building Essential** of "Goodness" through true-faith in the Most High Heavenly Father is used to overcome and resist the **9th of the 9 Deadly Venoms of the Desires of the great dragon, that old serpent called the devil and satan which deceiveth the whole world** known as "**Wickedness**" by learning and practicing goodness, uprightness of heart and life, kindness, and the virtue of beneficence (**Goodness - ἀγαθωσύνη Agathōsýnē**) every day."

93

"And whatsoever we ask, we receive of him,
because we keep his commandments, and do those
things that are pleasing in his sight, KJV 1 John 3:22."

Beware of the Pink Assassin (Your Tongue): The True Vine
(Yashu'a, Jesus) Power of Life and Death is in the Tongue;
Speaking God's (אלהים Elohîym) "Will"
for Your Life into Existence!

CHILDREN OF THE MOST HIGH:
PRISTINE YOUTH AND FAMILY SOLUTIONS, LLC.
SONS AND DAUGHTERS OF THE MOST HIGH PUBLISHERS ®

*Oh, Gracious Most High Heavenly father, Holy is your name,
Your Will Be Done Now and Forever!*

7: "**Faith** - πίστις **Pístis**, pis'-tis; from KJV Bible Greek
Strong's Concordance **#3982**; which means: **persuasion**, i.e.
credence; **moral conviction** (of religious truth, or the
truthfulness of God or a religious teacher), especially reliance
upon Christ for salvation; abstractly, constancy in such
profession; by extension, the system of religious (Gospel) truth
itself: —assurance, belief, believe, faith, fidelity. In KJV bible
book of Galatians chapter 5 verse 22; it states: "But the fruit of
the Spirit is love, joy, peace, longsuffering, gentleness,
goodness, **faith**." The **True Vine Yashu'a (Jesus) Fruit of the
Spirit of Positive Character-Building Essential** of "Faith"
through true-faith in the Most High Heavenly Father is used to
overcome and resist the **6th of the 9 Deadly Venoms of the
Desires of the great dragon, that old serpent called the devil
and satan which deceiveth the whole world** known as
"Hopeless-Fear- Disobedience" by learning and practicing
true-faith (Faith - πίστις Pístis)" in the Most High heavenly
Father through the Messiah Yashu'a (Jesus). "**Hopeless Fear
Disobedience**" are rooted in a lack of faith in the Most High
Heavenly Father. Real fear is the lack of true-faith in the Most
High Heavenly Father.

94

**"And whatsoever we ask, we receive of him,
because we keep his commandments, and do those
things that are pleasing in his sight, KJV 1 John 3:22."**

Beware of the Pink Assassin (Your Tongue): The True Vine (Yashu'a, Jesus) Power of Life and Death is in the Tongue; Speaking God's (אלהים Elŏhîym) "Will" for Your Life into Existence!

CHILDREN OF THE MOST HIGH:
PRISTINE YOUTH AND FAMILY SOLUTIONS, LLC.
SONS AND DAUGHTERS OF THE MOST HIGH PUBLISHERS ®

Oh, Gracious Most High Heavenly father, Holy is your name, Your Will Be Done Now and Forever!

8: "<u>Meekness</u> - πραότης praiótēs, **prah-ot'-ace**; which means: **gentleness, mildness by implication, humility**. In KJV bible book of Galatians chapter 5 verse 23; it states: "**Meekness, temperance: against such there is no law.**" The **True Vine Yashu'a (Jesus) Fruit of the Spirit of Positive Character-Building Essential** of "**Meekness**" through true-faith in the Most High Heavenly Father is used to overcome and resist the **3rd of the 9 Deadly Venoms of the Desires of the great dragon, that old serpent called the devil and satan which deceiveth the whole world** known as "**Pride**" by learning and practicing **Meekness** - πραότης **praiótēs true-faith (Faith - πίστις Pístis)** which overcomes pride."

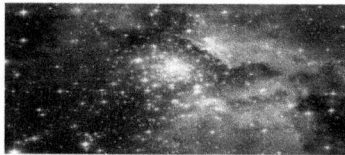

95

"And whatsoever we ask, we receive of him, because we keep his commandments, and do those things that are pleasing in his sight, KJV 1 John 3:22."

Beware of the Pink Assassin (Your Tongue): The True Vine
(Yashu'a, Jesus) Power of Life and Death is in the Tongue;
Speaking God's (אלהים Elõhîym) "Will"
for Your Life into Existence!

CHILDREN OF THE MOST HIGH:
PRISTINE YOUTH AND FAMILY SOLUTIONS, LLC.
SONS AND DAUGHTERS OF THE MOST HIGH PUBLISHERS ®

Oh, Gracious Most High Heavenly father, Holy is your name,
Your Will Be Done Now and Forever!

9: "**Temperance** ἐγκράτεια **Enkráteia, eng-krat'-i-ah**; from KJV Bible Strong's Greek **#G1468**; which means: **self-control** (especially continence): temperance. Self-control (the virtue of one who masters his or her desires and passions, esp. his sensual appetites). In KJV bible book of Galatians chapter 5 verse 23; it states: "Meekness, **temperance**: against such there is no law." The **True Vine Yashu'a (Jesus) Fruit of the Spirit of Positive Character-Building Essential** of "Temperance" through true-faith in the Most High Heavenly Father is used to overcome and resist the **4th of the 9 Deadly Venoms of the Desires of the great dragon, that old serpent called the devil and satan which deceiveth the whole world** known as "**Greed**" by learning and practicing self-control which is the virtue of one who masters his or her desires and passions every day, (Hughes, 2019).

96

"And whatsoever we ask, we receive of him, because we keep his commandments, and do those things that are pleasing in his sight, KJV 1 John 3:22."

Beware of the Pink Assassin (Your Tongue): The True Vine (Yashu'a, Jesus) Power of Life and Death is in the Tongue; Speaking God's (אלהים Elôhíym) "Will" for Your Life into Existence!

CHILDREN OF THE MOST HIGH:
PRISTINE YOUTH AND FAMILY SOLUTIONS, LLC.
SONS AND DAUGHTERS OF THE MOST HIGH PUBLISHERS ®

Oh, Gracious Most High Heavenly father, Holy is your name, Your Will Be Done Now and Forever!

So, the Love Words that are rooted in the Foundation of the True Vine (Yashu'a, Jesus) Fruits of the Spirit of Positive Character-Building Essentials are: <u>love</u>, <u>joy</u>, <u>peace</u>, <u>longsuffering</u>, <u>gentleness</u>, <u>goodness</u>, <u>faith</u>, <u>Meekness</u>, <u>temperance</u>. According Newberg and Walman (2012), "A single word has the power to influence the expression of genes that regulate the physical and emotional stress."

97

"And whatsoever we ask, we receive of him, because we keep his commandments, and do those things that are pleasing in his sight, KJV 1 John 3:22."

Beware of the Pink Assassin (Your Tongue): The True Vine
(Yashu'a, Jesus) Power of Life and Death is in the Tongue;
Speaking God's (אלהים Elóhîym) "Will"
for Your Life into Existence!

*Oh, Gracious Most High Heavenly father, Holy is your name,
Your Will Be Done Now and Forever!*

Also, Dr. Newberg neurological research indicates that words can change your brain (Newberg and Walman, 2012). Therefore; we must incorporate these **love words**, **their meanings**, and **their synonyms into our minds**, **hearts**, and **into our everyday communications**. **The children of the Most High must continuously put the following words in A.C.T.I.O.N. (Activated, Consciousness, Timely, Intentions, Obligated, Now) through all of our works, and in all that we are graciously blessed with the opportunity to do**: "On my own accord, I can of mine own self do nothing, I seek not mine own will, but the will of the Father which hath sent me" according to the Most High Heavenly Father's pre**ordained purpose** for your life." **By thinking, saying, and doing the aforementioned; you can be very successful at Mind Gardening in the Creative Garden of Will (Your Mind) to grow the habit of speaking the True Vine (Yashu'a, Jesus) Power of Life INTO EXISTENCE by the "Will" of the Most High Heavenly Father for your life!**

98
**"And whatsoever we ask, we receive of him,
because we keep his commandments, and do those
things that are pleasing in his sight, KJV 1 John 3:22."**

Beware of the Pink Assassin (Your Tongue): The True Vine (Yashu'a, Jesus) Power of Life and Death is in the Tongue; Speaking God's (אלהים Elóhîym) "Will" for Your Life into Existence!

CHILDREN OF THE MOST HIGH:
PRISTINE YOUTH AND FAMILY SOLUTIONS, LLC.
SONS AND DAUGHTERS OF THE MOST HIGH PUBLISHERS ®

Oh, Gracious Most High Heavenly father, Holy is your name, Your Will Be Done Now and Forever!

Chapter 5: <u>Developing the Habit of Only Speaking through the Portion of the Most High that exists in each of us</u>, Like the True-Vine (Yashu'a, Jesus) did! Thoughts, Words, Meditation, True-Prayer, and Mind Gardening Memorization Keys to Success!

"For that ye ought to say, If the Lord will, we shall live, and do this, or that (KJV bible James 4:15)."

99

"And whatsoever we ask, we receive of him, because we keep his commandments, and do those things that are pleasing in his sight, KJV 1 John 3:22."

Beware of the Pink Assassin (Your Tongue): The True Vine
(Yashu'a, Jesus) Power of Life and Death is in the Tongue;
Speaking God's (אלהים Elŏhîym) "Will"
for Your Life into Existence!

CHILDREN OF THE MOST HIGH:
PRISTINE YOUTH AND FAMILY SOLUTIONS, LLC.
SONS AND DAUGHTERS OF THE MOST HIGH PUBLISHERS ®

Oh, Gracious Most High Heavenly father, Holy is your name,
Your Will Be Done Now and Forever!

In the KJV bible book of Matthew chapter 22 verses 34-40; its states: "But when the Pharisees had heard that he had put the Sadducees to silence, they were gathered together. Then one of them, which was a lawyer, asked him a question, tempting him, and saying, **Master, which is the great commandment in the law**? Jesus said unto him, "Thou shalt love the Lord thy God with all thy heart, and with all thy soul, and with all thy mind. This is the first and great commandment. And the second is like unto it, Thou shalt love thy neighbour as thyself. On these two commandments hang all the law and the prophets." **If your heart is filled with love for the Most High and the Messiah Yashu'a (Jesus), who is being Interpreted as the Christ (KJV John 1:41); you will be able to develop the Habit of Only Speaking through the Portion of the Most High that exists in each of us, like the True-Vine (Yashu'a, Jesus) did in due time**!

100

**"And whatsoever we ask, we receive of him,
because we keep his commandments, and do those
things that are pleasing in his sight, KJV 1 John 3:22."**

Beware of the Pink Assassin (Your Tongue): The True Vine
(Yashu'a, Jesus) Power of Life and Death is in the Tongue;
Speaking God's (אלהים Elŏhîym) "Will"
for Your Life into Existence!

CHILDREN OF THE MOST HIGH:
PRISTINE YOUTH AND FAMILY SOLUTIONS, LLC.
SONS AND DAUGHTERS OF THE MOST HIGH PUBLISHERS ®

Oh, Gracious Most High Heavenly father, Holy is your name,
Your Will Be Done Now and Forever!

In the KJV bible book of Hosea chapter 10 verse 16-17; it states:
"This is **the covenant** (διαθήκη **Diathēkē (Dee-ath-ay'-kay)** –
means: **a contract (especially a devisory will):—covenant,
testament**) that I will make with them after those days, **saith
the Lord** (κύριος Kyrios), **I will put my laws into their
hearts, and in their minds will I write them**. And **their sins
and iniquities will I remember no more**." Thereby, if **the
Lord** (κύριος Kyrios), **put his laws into our hearts, and in
our minds**; this will influence how the children of the Most
High **thinks and feels**, and how we **learn the invaluableness
of the words we think, speak, and internalize; correlates to
our overall health and wellbeing!** This is essential, in order
for the children of the Most High to develop the habit of
speaking **Life (Positivity)** instead of **Death (Negativity)** into
existence through the **Power of our Tongues!**

**"And whatsoever we ask, we receive of him,
because we keep his commandments, and do those
things that are pleasing in his sight, KJV 1 John 3:22."**

Beware of the Pink Assassin (Your Tongue): The True Vine (Yashu'a, Jesus) Power of Life and Death is in the Tongue; **Speaking God's (אלהים Elóhîym) "Will" for Your Life into Existence!**

CHILDREN OF THE MOST HIGH:
PRISTINE YOUTH AND FAMILY SOLUTIONS, LLC.
SONS AND DAUGHTERS OF THE MOST HIGH PUBLISHERS ®

Oh, Gracious Most High Heavenly father, Holy is your name, Your Will Be Done Now and Forever!

In the Online KJV bible Greek Strong's Concordance (2020), "**the Word** (λόγος **Logos**)" in the book of John chapter 1 verse 1, has a multitude of in-depth meanings as mentioned in chapter 1 of this book. For this chapter, "**the Word** (λόγος **Logos**) utilizes "**the Word** (λόγος **Logos**)" definitions of: **Thoughts, Words, Meditation**" which works with <u>**True Prayer Supplication**</u> in the Developing the Habit of Only Speaking through the Portion of the Most High that exists in each of us!

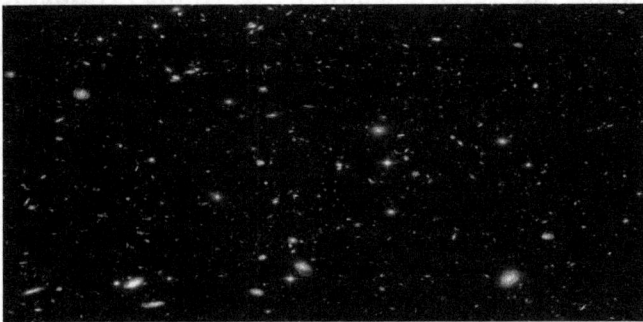

102

"And whatsoever we ask, we receive of him, because we keep his commandments, and do those things that are pleasing in his sight, KJV 1 John 3:22."

Beware of the Pink Assassin (Your Tongue): The True Vine (Yashu'a, Jesus) Power of Life and Death is in the Tongue; Speaking God's (אלהים Elohîym) "Will" for Your Life into Existence!

CHILDREN OF THE MOST HIGH:
PRISTINE YOUTH AND FAMILY SOLUTIONS, LLC.
SONS AND DAUGHTERS OF THE MOST HIGH PUBLISHERS ®

Oh, Gracious Most High Heavenly father, Holy is your name, Your Will Be Done Now and Forever!

True-Prayer Supplication occurs through the combination of **spoken words** from a sincere heart and intentionally, **concentrated mind that is focused on the Most High only,** and through the **daily internal practicing of meditation**. This occurs by us willingly, allowing **the Most High's words and laws** to be **placed in our hearts and in our minds**. **When this occurs, it puts our minds in alignment** with the "Will" of the Most High as stated in the KJV bible book of Hebrews chapter 8 verse 10; it states: "For this is the covenant that I will make with the house of Israel after those days, saith the Lord; I will put my laws into their mind, and write them in their hearts: and I will be to them a God, and they shall be to me a people." Thus, **when we pray the Most High's words, and obey the Most High's laws that are placed in our hearts and minds**, the Most High's "Will", **becomes our will**.

103

"And whatsoever we ask, we receive of him, because we keep his commandments, and do those things that are pleasing in his sight, KJV 1 John 3:22."

Beware of the Pink Assassin (Your Tongue): The True Vine
(Yashu'a, Jesus) Power of Life and Death is in the Tongue;
Speaking God's (אלהים Elóhîym) "Will"
for Your Life into Existence!

CHILDREN OF THE MOST HIGH:
PRISTINE YOUTH AND FAMILY SOLUTIONS, LLC.
SONS AND DAUGHTERS OF THE MOST HIGH PUBLISHERS ®

Oh, Gracious Most High Heavenly father, Holy is your name,
Your Will Be Done Now and Forever!

Our True-Prayer Supplications must be directed through the portion of the Most High that exists in us as stated in the KJV bible book of John chapter 1 verses 1-5. However, this should not ever be misinterpreted as praying to yourself as the Most High (**that would be BLASPHEMY!**). In the KJV bible book of John chapter 1 verses 1-5; it states: "In the beginning was **the Word**, and **the Word** was with God, and **the Word** was God. **The same was in the beginning** with God. All things were made by him; and without him was not anything made that was made."

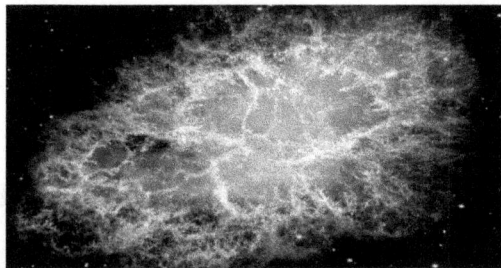

104

"And whatsoever we ask, we receive of him, because we keep his commandments, and do those things that are pleasing in his sight, KJV 1 John 3:22."

Beware of the Pink Assassin (Your Tongue): The True Vine
(Yashu'a, Jesus) Power of Life and Death is in the Tongue;
Speaking God's (אלהים Eloʹhiym) "Will"
for Your Life into Existence!

CHILDREN OF THE MOST HIGH:
PRISTINE YOUTH AND FAMILY SOLUTIONS, LLC.
SONS AND DAUGHTERS OF THE MOST HIGH PUBLISHERS ®

Oh, Gracious Most High Heavenly father, Holy is your name,
Your Will Be Done Now and Forever!

"In him was <u>life</u> (**breath of life from the Lord God**); and <u>the</u>
<u>life</u> (**from the Lord God made people into living souls**) was
the light (<u>**Neshamaw Khayyeem**</u> נשמה חײם - **Divine Breath of**
Life) of men (human beings). And the light (**<u>portion of the</u>**
<u>Most High that exists in every person</u>) shineth in darkness (**<u>is</u>**
<u>inside the body of every person</u>); and the darkness (**the body**
and <u>the mind</u> in many people lack of the knowledge of how
a portion of the Most High exists in every person)
<u>comprehended it not</u>." So, there is a portion of the Most High
Heavenly Father which is a: "**Spiritual Majesty**" that exists in
each person that is dormant in many of us. **Spiritual Majesty**
it is a portion of the Most High that exists in each person which
is usually not allowed to function in our lives due to many of us
living most days according to other people plans of how they
want us to utilize our limited time, and limited energy on other
people plans for our lives that may not have our best interest;
rather than becoming aware of the Most High's pre-ordained
plan for each of our lives, stop wasting time, and learning how
to best, only live by the "**Will**" and commandments of the Most
High (Hughes, 2019).

105

"And whatsoever we ask, we receive of him,
because we keep his commandments, and do those
things that are pleasing in his sight, KJV 1 John 3:22."

Beware of the Pink Assassin (Your Tongue): The True Vine (Yashu'a, Jesus) Power of Life and Death is in the Tongue; Speaking God's (אלהים Elohîym) "Will" for Your Life into Existence!

CHILDREN OF THE MOST HIGH:
PRISTINE YOUTH AND FAMILY SOLUTIONS, LLC.
SONS AND DAUGHTERS OF THE MOST HIGH PUBLISHERS ®

Oh, Gracious Most High Heavenly father, Holy is your name, Your Will Be Done Now and Forever!

Spiritual Majesty is an inner quality that when it is intentionally organized and directed towards positive accomplishments it activates our higher potential that helps us to conquer adverse situations. Also, when our **Spiritual Majesty** is intentionally organized and directed towards positive accomplishments, it activates the ability to create positive life achievements that afford us the opportunity to get more out of life by sacrificing through our works in a positive healthy manner to give more to life. So, the most important aspect of **True-Prayer Supplication** is <u>**Developing the Habit of Only Speaking through the Portion of the Most High that exists in each of us, combined with Meditation and Prayer.**</u> <u>**Mediation**</u> is the art of <u>**listening and not speaking**</u>. <u>**Prayer**</u> is the art of <u>**speaking**</u> to the unseen and <u>**not listening**</u>.

106
"And whatsoever we ask, we receive of him, because we keep his commandments, and do those things that are pleasing in his sight, KJV 1 John 3:22."

Beware of the Pink Assassin (Your Tongue): The True Vine (Yashu'a, Jesus) Power of Life and Death is in the Tongue; Speaking God's (אלהים Elóhîym) "Will" for Your Life into Existence!

CHILDREN OF THE MOST HIGH:
PRISTINE YOUTH AND FAMILY SOLUTIONS, LLC.
SONS AND DAUGHTERS OF THE MOST HIGH PUBLISHERS ®

Oh, Gracious Most High Heavenly father, Holy is your name, Your Will Be Done Now and Forever!

An Example of a <u>Meditative Thought is</u>: "<u>Oh Most Gracious Most High Heavenly Father, Holy is your Name, Your Will Be Done</u>." In the KJV bible book of Mathew chapter 6 verses 9-10; Yashu'a (Jesus) **said**: "After this manner therefore <u>pray</u> ye: Our Father which art in heaven, hallowed (ἁγιάζω **Hagiazō means Holy**) be thy name. Thy kingdom come. <u>Thy will be done</u> in earth, as it is in heaven."

What is True-Faith?

<u>True-Faith is unshakable moral conviction of the truth and trust in the Most High Heavenly Father, the Messiah Yashu'a (Jesus), the Most High Heavenly Father's Angelic-Beings who are Messengers of the Most High and who are sent to certain members of humanity to teach us how to obey the Most High's laws, commandments, and to learn and teach the Most High's Doctrine only</u>.

107

"And whatsoever we ask, we receive of him, because we keep his commandments, and do those things that are pleasing in his sight, KJV 1 John 3:22."

Beware of the Pink Assassin (Your Tongue): The True Vine
(Yashu'a, Jesus) Power of Life and Death is in the Tongue;
Speaking God's (אלהים Elóhîym) "Will"
for Your Life into Existence!

*Oh, Gracious Most High Heavenly father, Holy is your name,
Your Will Be Done Now and Forever!*

When the previous verse mentions to only do the Most High
Heavenly Father's "**Will**" (**Thy Will Be Done**) on earth as it is
in **heaven** (the word "**heaven**" is the KJV bible Greek Strong's
Concordance "**#3772 word: οὐρανός Ouranos. Ouranos is the
Greek word for the English word "Orion" in reference to the
Orion Star Constellation. Not to be mistaken for the
Kingdom of God. Heaven (Ouranos) is in the Kingdom of
God**. In the **KJV bible book of Job chapter 9 verse 9**; it states:
"Which maketh **Arcturus**, **Orion**, and **Pleiades**, and the
chambers of the south." These are Star Constellations created
by the Most High Heavenly Father. That's why in the KJV
bible book of John chapter 14 verse 2; Yashu'a (Jesus) said: "In
my Father's house [**throughout the boundless universes** and
outside the boundless universes] are many mansions (the
KJV bible Greek Strong's Concordance word for "**mansions**"
is the word: **μονή Monē** which means: a staying, abiding,
dwelling, abode): if it were not so, I would have told you. I
go to prepare a place for you."

108

**"And whatsoever we ask, we receive of him,
because we keep his commandments, and do those
things that are pleasing in his sight, KJV 1 John 3:22."**

Beware of the Pink Assassin (Your Tongue): The True Vine
(Yashu'a, Jesus) Power of Life and Death is in the Tongue;
Speaking God's (אלהים Elŏhîym) "Will"
for Your Life into Existence!

CHILDREN OF THE MOST HIGH:
PRISTINE YOUTH AND FAMILY SOLUTIONS, LLC.
SONS AND DAUGHTERS OF THE MOST HIGH PUBLISHERS ®

*Oh, Gracious Most High Heavenly father, Holy is your name,
Your Will Be Done Now and Forever!*

What do you mean when you say: "outside the boundless
universes?" We mean that **Existence predates Creation.** In
order for the Most High Heavenly Father to have **created the
boundless universes, the Most High Heavenly Father had to
exist before the creation of all that was created.** The Most
High Heavenly Father is the **Creator of all creators** and
existed outside of creation during the time that the **sum of
things** or that which **adds up to something** were being created.
Also, **True-Faith must be grounded in substantiated facts
that are strongly supported through, evidence, experience
and reason.**

109
**"And whatsoever we ask, we receive of him,
because we keep his commandments, and do those
things that are pleasing in his sight, KJV 1 John 3:22."**

Beware of the Pink Assassin (Your Tongue): The True Vine (Yashu'a, Jesus) Power of Life and Death is in the Tongue; Speaking God's (אלהים Elohîym) "Will" for Your Life into Existence!

CHILDREN OF THE MOST HIGH:
PRISTINE YOUTH AND FAMILY SOLUTIONS, LLC.
SONS AND DAUGHTERS OF THE MOST HIGH PUBLISHERS ®

Oh, Gracious Most High Heavenly father, Holy is your name, Your Will Be Done Now and Forever!

According to the children of the Most High, is the Creative Garden of Will (Your Mind) like a Magic Garden? Yes. How? Each person plants **mental seeds (thoughts)** in their **Creative Garden of Will (Your Mind) with each thought (mental seed)** that they have. The **Creative Garden of Will (Your Mind) is like a Magic Garden** because any **mental seeds (thoughts)** you plant in the **Creative Garden of Will (Your Mind)**, they will grow. If you put **poison mental seeds (negative thoughts)** in it, they will grow. If you put **positive mental seeds (positive thoughts)** in it, they will grow. Therefore; **thoughts and words matter, and thoughts proceed all words** as it relates to **the True Vine (Yashu'a, Jesus) Power of Life and Death that is in the Tongue, being SPOKEN INTO EXISTENCE by the "Will" of the Most High Heavenly Father for your life!**

110

"And whatsoever we ask, we receive of him, because we keep his commandments, and do those things that are pleasing in his sight, KJV 1 John 3:22."

Beware of the Pink Assassin (Your Tongue): The True Vine
(Yashu'a, Jesus) Power of Life and Death is in the Tongue;
Speaking God's (אלהים Elŏhîym) "Will"
for Your Life into Existence!

CHILDREN OF THE MOST HIGH:
PRISTINE YOUTH AND FAMILY SOLUTIONS, LLC.
SONS AND DAUGHTERS OF THE MOST HIGH PUBLISHERS ®

Oh, Gracious Most High Heavenly father, Holy is your name,
Your Will Be Done Now and Forever!

According to (Hughes, 2019); "The **1st of the 9 True Vine
(Yashu'a, Jesus) B.A.-K.A.-R.E.** Sequential Order of
Learning Habits of Success, that introduces **the mind to
thoughts that give birth to new ideas**; are the **9 True Vine
(Yashu'a, Jesus) Mind Gardening Memorization Keys to
Success** that may help a person" **to grow the habit of speaking
the True Vine (Yashu'a, Jesus) Power of Life INTO
EXISTENCE by the "Will" of the Most High Heavenly
Father for your life**, are:

1. Glorify the Most High Heavenly Father through the Messiah
   Yashu'a (Jesus).

2. Apply the Most High's Scriptural Knowledge in all that you do.

3. Revere the Most High and have moral reverence for the Most
   High.

**"And whatsoever we ask, we receive of him,
because we keep his commandments, and do those
things that are pleasing in his sight, KJV 1 John 3:22."**

Beware of the Pink Assassin (Your Tongue): The True Vine
(Yashu'a, Jesus) Power of Life and Death is in the Tongue;
Speaking God's (אלהים Elōhíym) "Will"
for Your Life into Existence!

CHILDREN OF THE MOST HIGH:
PRISTINE YOUTH AND FAMILY SOLUTIONS, LLC.
SONS AND DAUGHTERS OF THE MOST HIGH PUBLISHERS ®

*Oh, Gracious Most High Heavenly father, Holy is your name,
Your Will Be Done Now and Forever!*

4. **D**ecrease so that the Messiah Yashu'a (Jesus) can increase within you.

5. **E**xcept a person be born again, he or she cannot see the kingdom of the Most High.

6. **N**ourish yourself and others with the Most High's Scriptural Knowledge.

7. **I**nform yourself and others about the Most High's Scriptural Knowledge.

8. **N**arrow is the way that leads unto eternal life through the Messiah Yashu'a (Jesus).

9. **G**race and truth came by way of the Messiah Yashu'a (Jesus).

112

**"And whatsoever we ask, we receive of him,
because we keep his commandments, and do those
things that are pleasing in his sight, KJV 1 John 3:22."**

Beware of the Pink Assassin (Your Tongue): The True Vine (Yashu'a, Jesus) Power of Life and Death is in the Tongue; Speaking God's (אלהים Elồhîym) "Will" for Your Life into Existence!

CHILDREN OF THE MOST HIGH:
PRISTINE YOUTH AND FAMILY SOLUTIONS, LLC.
SONS AND DAUGHTERS OF THE MOST HIGH PUBLISHERS ®

Oh, Gracious Most High Heavenly father, Holy is your name,
Your Will Be Done Now and Forever!

Explain how the 9 True Vine (Yashu'a, Jesus) Mind Gardening Memorization Keys to Success concept of **Gardening**, relates to Mind Gardening and its relationship to the Most High, the True Vine (the Messiah Yashu'a, Jesus), the branches, obeying the laws of the Most High, mind, heart, and grace? The **Most High Heavenly Father is the Creator** of the **Mind** and on a **macro level from the people on earth viewpoint, the Boundless Universes combined may be one of the Most High's Garden's**, (Hughes, 2019). The Messiah Yashu'a (Jesus) is **the True Vine** as stated in the KJV bible book of John chapter 15 verse 1; he said: "I am the true vine, and my Father is the husbandman." The children of the Most High who accept the Messiah Yashu'a (Jesus) into their **hearts** as their savior, will be **the branches** as Yashu'a (Jesus) said in the KJV bible book of John chapter 15 verse 4; he said: (I am the vine, ye are the branches: He that abideth in me, and I in him, the same bringeth forth much fruit: for without me ye can do nothing)."

113

"And whatsoever we ask, we receive of him, because we keep his commandments, and do those things that are pleasing in his sight, KJV 1 John 3:22."

Beware of the Pink Assassin (Your Tongue): The True Vine
(Yashu'a, Jesus) Power of Life and Death is in the Tongue;
**Speaking God's (אלהים Elóhîym) "Will"
for Your Life into Existence!**

CHILDREN OF THE MOST HIGH:
PRISTINE YOUTH AND FAMILY SOLUTIONS, LLC.
SONS AND DAUGHTERS OF THE MOST HIGH PUBLISHERS ®

*Oh, Gracious Most High Heavenly father, Holy is your name,
Your Will Be Done Now and Forever!*

Growth occurs over time by learning and obeying the laws of
the Most High which initiates all thoughts through the
activating of the "**Will**" of the Most High Heavenly Father in
the minds of the children of the Most High. Once this occurs,
Yashu'a (Jesus) makes them into **Mind Gardeners** who
become practitioners of **Mind Gardening**! In the KJV bible
book of Hebrews chapter 10 verse 16; it states: "**This is the
covenant that I will make with them after those days, saith
the Lord, I will put my laws into their hearts, and in their
minds will I write them.**" In the KJV bible book of Revelation
chapter 22 verse 14; it states: "Blessed are they that do his
commandments, that they may have right to the tree of life, and
may enter in through the gates into the city."

114
**"And whatsoever we ask, we receive of him,
because we keep his commandments, and do those
things that are pleasing in his sight, KJV 1 John 3:22."**

Beware of the Pink Assassin (Your Tongue): The True Vine
(Yashu'a, Jesus) Power of Life and Death is in the Tongue;
Speaking God's (אלהים Elŏhîym) "Will"
for Your Life into Existence!

CHILDREN OF THE MOST HIGH:
PRISTINE YOUTH AND FAMILY SOLUTIONS, LLC.
SONS AND DAUGHTERS OF THE MOST HIGH PUBLISHERS ®

Oh, Gracious Most High Heavenly father, Holy is your name,
Your Will Be Done Now and Forever!

As it relates to **Mind Gardening, what does the heart have to do with the mind and words**? In the KJV bible book of Matthew chapter 15 verse 8; the Messiah Yashu'a (Jesus) said: "Those things [**words**] which proceed out of the mouth come forth from the heart; and they defile a person." As a necessary essential, **to grow the habit of speaking the True Vine (Yashu'a, Jesus) Power of Life INTO EXISTENCE by the "Will" of the Most High Heavenly Father for your life**, a person must have a clean or pure heart that is forgiven of all sins through repentance which is why the Messiah Yashu'a (Jesus) stands at the door of the **hearts** of people offering **grace**, **truth** (KJV bible book of John chapter 1 verse 17) and **eternal life**. The Messiah Yashu'a (Jesus) said in the KJV bible book of Revelation chapter 3 verse 20; he said: "Behold, I stand at the door, and knock: if any man [person] hear my voice, and open the door [of the **heart**], I will come in to him, and will sup with him [or her], and he [or she] with me."

115

"And whatsoever we ask, we receive of him, because we keep his commandments, and do those things that are pleasing in his sight, KJV 1 John 3:22."

Beware of the Pink Assassin (Your Tongue): The True Vine
(Yashu'a, Jesus) Power of Life and Death is in the Tongue;
Speaking God's (אלהים Elóhîym) "Will"
for Your Life into Existence!

CHILDREN OF THE MOST HIGH:
PRISTINE YOUTH AND FAMILY SOLUTIONS, LLC.
SONS AND DAUGHTERS OF THE MOST HIGH PUBLISHERS ®

*Oh, Gracious Most High Heavenly father, Holy is your name,
Your Will Be Done Now and Forever!*

"The word "**Grace**" is the KJV bible Greek Strong's
Concordance #5485 word: χάρις **Charis** (**Khar`-ece**), which
means graciousness (as gratifying), of manner or act (abstract
or concrete; literal, figurative or spiritual; especially the divine
influence upon the heart, and its reflection in the life; including
gratitude): acceptable, benefit, favor, gift, grace(- ious), joy,
liberality, pleasure, thank(-s, -worthy)." This is why the
Messiah Yashu'a (Jesus) said in the KJV bible book of Matthew
chapter 6 verse 21; he said: "For where your treasure is, there
will your heart be also." **Therefore; allowing the Most High
to divide the disagreeable from agreeable in our hearts is
essential to growing the habit of speaking the True Vine
(Yashu'a, Jesus) Power of Life INTO EXISTENCE by the
"Will" of the Most High Heavenly Father <u>for your life</u>!**

116
**"And whatsoever we ask, we receive of him,
because we keep his commandments, and do those
things that are pleasing in his sight, KJV 1 John 3:22."**

Beware of the Pink Assassin (Your Tongue): The True Vine (Yashu'a, Jesus) Power of Life and Death is in the Tongue; Speaking God's (אלהים Elohîym) "Will" for Your Life into Existence!

CHILDREN OF THE MOST HIGH:
PRISTINE YOUTH AND FAMILY SOLUTIONS, LLC.
SONS AND DAUGHTERS OF THE MOST HIGH PUBLISHERS ®

Oh, Gracious Most High Heavenly father, Holy is your name, Your Will Be Done Now and Forever!

Explain the 9 True Vine Yashu'a (Jesus) Mind Gardening Memorization Keys to Success of <u>Gardening</u> as it relates to the Mind Gardening from the Original language of the Bible verses where they come from? The 9 True Vine (Yashu'a, Jesus) Memorization Keys to Success acronyms of **<u>Gardening</u>** as it relates to the True Vine Yashu'a (Jesus) Mind Gardening from the original language that the Bible verses were revealed in is listed below:

1. <u>G</u>lorify – In the KJV bible book of Matthew chapter 5 verse 16; Yashu'a (Jesus) said: "Let your light so shine before men, that they may see your good works, and glorify your Father which is in heaven." In this verse, the word for "**glorify**", is the KJV bible Greek Strong's Concordance#1392 word: δοξάζω **Doxazo (Dox-ad`-zo)**, which means to render (or esteem) glorious (in a wide application): (make) glorify(-ious), full of (have) glory, honor, magnify.

117

"And whatsoever we ask, we receive of him, because we keep his commandments, and do those things that are pleasing in his sight, KJV 1 John 3:22."

Beware of the Pink Assassin (Your Tongue): The True Vine
(Yashu'a, Jesus) Power of Life and Death is in the Tongue;
**Speaking God's (אלהים Elŏhîym) "Will"
for Your Life into Existence!**

CHILDREN OF THE MOST HIGH:
PRISTINE YOUTH AND FAMILY SOLUTIONS, LLC.
SONS AND DAUGHTERS OF THE MOST HIGH PUBLISHERS ®

*Oh, Gracious Most High Heavenly father, Holy is your name,
Your Will Be Done Now and Forever!*

2. Apply - In the KJV bible book of Psalms chapter 90 verse 12;
   it states: "So teach us to number our days, **that we may apply**
   our hearts unto wisdom." In this verse, the KJV bible Hebrew
   Strong's Concordance#**935** word: בּוֹא **Bow' (Bō)**, which is the
   word for the phrase "**that we may apply**" which means to
   apply, attain, get, follow."

3. Revere or Reverence – In the KJV bible book of Proverbs
   chapter 1 verse 7; it states: "**The fear of the LORD is the
   beginning of knowledge: but fools** אֱוִיל **'Eviyl** (the phrase:
   "**but fools**" is KJV bible Hebrew Strong's Concordance #**191**
   word "**Ev·ēl**'" meaning to be perverse, evil, be foolish, foolish,
   of one who despises wisdom, of one who mocks when guilty,
   of one who is quarrelsome, of one who is licentious silly: fool(-
   ish). **despise wisdom and instruction**." In this verse, the word
   for "**fear**" is the KJV bible Hebrew Strong's Concordance
   #**3374** word: יִרְאָה **Yir'ah (Yir·ä')**, which means to "**fear**", to
   respect, reverence, piety revered respect, having moral
   reverence."

118
**"And whatsoever we ask, we receive of him,
because we keep his commandments, and do those
things that are pleasing in his sight, KJV 1 John 3:22."**

Beware of the Pink Assassin (Your Tongue): The True Vine
(Yashu'a, Jesus) Power of Life and Death is in the Tongue;
**Speaking God's (אלהים Elóhîym) "Will"
for Your Life into Existence!**

CHILDREN OF THE MOST HIGH:
PRISTINE YOUTH AND FAMILY SOLUTIONS, LLC.
SONS AND DAUGHTERS OF THE MOST HIGH PUBLISHERS ®

*Oh, Gracious Most High Heavenly father, Holy is your name,
Your Will Be Done Now and Forever!*

4. **D**ecrease – In the KJV bible book of John chapter 3 verse 30; it
states: "He must increase, but I **must decrease**." In this verse,
the word for the phrase "**must decrease**" is the KJV bible Greek
Strong's Concordance **#1642** word: ἐλαττόω **Elattoo (El-at-
to`-o)**, which means to lessen, make lower to make less or
inferior: in dignity, to be made less or inferior: in dignity; to
decrease in authority or popularity."

5. **E**xcept – In the KJV bible book of John chapter 3 verse 3;
Yashu'a (Jesus) said unto him: "Verily, verily, I say unto thee,
except a man be born again, he cannot see the kingdom of
God." In this verse, the word for "**except**" is the KJV bible
Greek Strong's Concordance #3362 word: ἐὰν μή **Ean mē (Eh-
an`-may)**, which means if not, unless, before, but, except.

**"And whatsoever we ask, we receive of him,
because we keep his commandments, and do those
things that are pleasing in his sight, KJV 1 John 3:22."**

Beware of the Pink Assassin (Your Tongue): The True Vine
(Yashu'a, Jesus) Power of Life and Death is in the Tongue;
**Speaking God's (אלהים Elohîym) "Will"
for Your Life into Existence!**

CHILDREN OF THE MOST HIGH:
PRISTINE YOUTH AND FAMILY SOLUTIONS, LLC.
SONS AND DAUGHTERS OF THE MOST HIGH PUBLISHERS ®

*Oh, Gracious Most High Heavenly father, Holy is your name,
Your Will Be Done Now and Forever!*

6. Nourish – In the KJV bible book of Genesis chapter 50 verse 21; it states: "Now therefore fear ye not: **I will nourish you**, and your little ones. And he comforted them, and spake kindly unto them." In this verse, the phrase for "**I will nourish you**" is the KJV bible Hebrew Strong's Concordance **#3557** word: כּוּל **Kuwl** (Kool), which means to maintain, sustain, provide sustenance."

7. Inform – In the KJV bible book of Deuteronomy chapter 17 verse 10; it states: "And thou shalt do according to the sentence, which they of that place which the LORD shall choose shall shew thee; and thou shalt observe to do **according to all that they inform** thee." In this verse, the phrase for "**according to all they inform**" is the KJV bible Hebrew Strong's Concordance **#3384** word: יָרָה **Yarah** (**Yaw-raw`**), which means to teach, direct, teach through, instruct, inform."

8. Narrow – In the KJV bible book of Matthew chapter 7 verse 14; Yashu'a (Jesus) said: "Because strait is the gate, and narrow is the way, which leadeth unto life, and few there be that find it." In this verse, the word for "**narrow**" is the KJV bible Greek King James Strong Concordance#2346 word: θλίβω **Thlibō** (**Thlee`-bo**), which means thin, tight, small width, slim, slender, limited in extent, amount, or scope; restricted, narrow."

120

**"And whatsoever we ask, we receive of him,
because we keep his commandments, and do those
things that are pleasing in his sight, KJV 1 John 3:22."**

Beware of the Pink Assassin (Your Tongue): The True Vine
(Yashu'a, Jesus) Power of Life and Death is in the Tongue;
Speaking God's (אלהים Elôhîym) "Will"
for Your Life into Existence!

CHILDREN OF THE MOST HIGH:
PRISTINE YOUTH AND FAMILY SOLUTIONS, LLC.
SONS AND DAUGHTERS OF THE MOST HIGH PUBLISHERS ®

Oh, Gracious Most High Heavenly father, Holy is your name,
Your Will Be Done Now and Forever!

9. <u>G</u>race – In the KJV bible book of Matthew chapter 1 verse 7; it
    stated: "For the law was given by Moses, but **grace** and truth
    came by Jesus Christ." In this verse, the word for "**grace**" is the
    KJV bible Greek King James Strong Concordance #5485 word:
    χάρις **Charis** (**Khä'-res**) means graciousness (as gratifying), of
    manner or act (abstract or concrete; literal, figurative or
    spiritual; especially the divine influence upon the heart, and its
    reflection in the life; including gratitude); acceptable, benefit,
    favor, gift, grace(- ious), joy, liberality, pleasure, thank(-s, -
    worthy)."

121
"And whatsoever we ask, we receive of him,
because we keep his commandments, and do those
things that are pleasing in his sight, KJV 1 John 3:22."

Beware of the Pink Assassin (Your Tongue): The True Vine
(Yashu'a, Jesus) Power of Life and Death is in the Tongue;
Speaking God's (אלהים Eloȟîym) "Will"
for Your Life into Existence!

CHILDREN OF THE MOST HIGH:
PRISTINE YOUTH AND FAMILY SOLUTIONS, LLC.
SONS AND DAUGHTERS OF THE MOST HIGH PUBLISHERS ®

Oh, Gracious Most High Heavenly father, Holy is your name,
Your Will Be Done Now and Forever!

So, our **Thoughts, Words, Meditation, True-Prayer Supplication, and Mind Gardening Memorization Keys to Success, are essential in** <u>**Developing the Habit of Only Speaking through the Portion of the Most High that exists in each of us,**</u> **Like the True-Vine (Yashu'a, Jesus) did!** Therefore; <u>**the children of the Most High must continuously put the following words in A.C.T.I.O.N. (Activated, Conscious, Timely, Intentions, Obligated, Now) through all of our works, and in all that we are graciously blessed with the opportunity to do**</u>: "On my own accord, I can of mine own self do nothing, I seek not mine own will, but the will of the Father which hath sent me" according to the Most High Heavenly Father's pre**ordained** **purpose** for your life." **By** <u>**thinking, saying, and doing the aforementioned; you can be very successful at**</u> **Mind Gardening in the Creative Garden of Will (Your Mind) to grow the habit of speaking the True Vine (Yashu'a, Jesus) Power of Life INTO EXISTENCE by the "Will" of the Most High Heavenly Father** <u>**for your life**</u>!

122

"And whatsoever we ask, we receive of him, because we keep his commandments, and do those things that are pleasing in his sight, KJV 1 John 3:22."

CHILDREN OF THE MOST HIGH:
PRISTINE YOUTH AND FAMILY SOLUTIONS, LLC.
SONS AND DAUGHTERS OF THE MOST HIGH PUBLISHERS ®

Oh, Gracious Most High Heavenly father, Holy is your name, Your Will Be Done Now and Forever!

Chapter 6: Idle Words, Idol Worship, Idolizing the Opposite of God, Worshiping Idly, and the Doctrine of the Most High! Speaking the **True-Vine (Yashu'a, Jesus) Truth** through **the Power of the Tongue to Kill Negative Habits!**

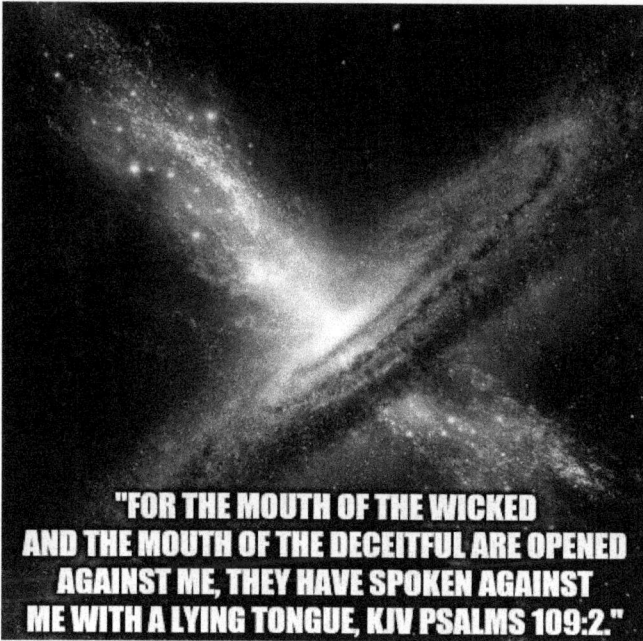

"FOR THE MOUTH OF THE WICKED AND THE MOUTH OF THE DECEITFUL ARE OPENED AGAINST ME, THEY HAVE SPOKEN AGAINST ME WITH A LYING TONGUE, KJV PSALMS 109:2."

123

"And whatsoever we ask, we receive of him, because we keep his commandments, and do those things that are pleasing in his sight, KJV 1 John 3:22."

CHILDREN OF THE MOST HIGH:
PRISTINE YOUTH AND FAMILY SOLUTIONS, LLC.
SONS AND DAUGHTERS OF THE MOST HIGH PUBLISHERS ®

Oh, Gracious Most High Heavenly father, Holy is your name,
Your Will Be Done Now and Forever!

In this chapter, we will utilize the Online KJV Blue Letter bible Greek Strong's Concordance (2020), "**the Word** (λόγος **Logos**) "**the Word** (λόγος **Logos**)" definition of: **Doctrine**, **Teaching**, and **Kind or Style of Speaking**" and the Thayer's Greek Bible Lexicon (2011) definition of "**the Word** (λόγος **Logos**)" being: **the doctrine concerning the attainment through Christ of salvation in the kingdom of God**, which are essential in **Developing the Habit the True Vine (Yashu'a, Jesus) Power of Life and Death in the Tongue, being SPOKEN INTO EXISTENCE by the "Will" of the Most High Heavenly Father for your life!**

124

"And whatsoever we ask, we receive of him, because we keep his commandments, and do those things that are pleasing in his sight, KJV 1 John 3:22."

Beware of the Pink Assassin (Your Tongue): The True Vine
(Yashu'a, Jesus) Power of Life and Death is in the Tongue;
Speaking God's (אלהים Elôhîym) "Will"
for Your Life into Existence!

CHILDREN OF THE MOST HIGH:
PRISTINE YOUTH AND FAMILY SOLUTIONS, LLC.
SONS AND DAUGHTERS OF THE MOST HIGH PUBLISHERS ®

Oh, Gracious Most High Heavenly father, Holy is your name,
Your Will Be Done Now and Forever!

When Speaking God's (אלהים Elôhîym) A.W.A.R.E. (All Wise Abundant Right Exact) Knowledge; what does the phrase: "Talking Behind My Back" REALLY Mean in Order to Speak the True Vine (Yashu'a, Jesus) Power of Life in the Tongue?

<u>**If SOMEONE WERE TALKING BEHIND YOUR BACK, THEY WOULD BE IN FRONT OF YOUR FACE, BECAUSE YOUR FACE IS BEHIND YOUR BACK!**</u>

Have you or someone that you know ever said: "Somebody or some people were talking behind my back? What does that phrase mean? Now, after looking at it with **God's (אלהים Elôhîym) A.W.A.R.E. (All Wise Abundant Right Exact) knowledge**, ask yourself; is your face on the front of your body? Or is your face and back on the same side of your body? Or is your back on the backside of your body and your face on the front side of your body?

125

"And whatsoever we ask, we receive of him, because we keep his commandments, and do those things that are pleasing in his sight, KJV 1 John 3:22."

Beware of the Pink Assassin (Your Tongue): The True Vine
(Yashu'a, Jesus) Power of Life and Death is in the Tongue;
Speaking God's (אלהים Elŏhîym) "Will"
for Your Life into Existence!

CHILDREN OF THE MOST HIGH:
PRISTINE YOUTH AND FAMILY SOLUTIONS, LLC.
SONS AND DAUGHTERS OF THE MOST HIGH PUBLISHERS ®

Oh, Gracious Most High Heavenly father, Holy is your name,
Your Will Be Done Now and Forever!

So, from a physical, biological perspective; if someone where
talking behind your back, they would literally be in front of your
face, because your face is behind your back! **If you can
literally, mentally; overstand that your face is behind your
back, and that if someone where talking behind your back,
they would literally be in front of your face. You can be very
successful at Mind Gardening in the Creative Garden of
Will (Your Mind) to grow the habit of speaking the True
Vine (Yashu'a, Jesus) Power of Life INTO EXISTENCE by
the "Will" of the Most High Heavenly Father for your life!**

126

**"And whatsoever we ask, we receive of him,
because we keep his commandments, and do those
things that are pleasing in his sight, KJV 1 John 3:22."**

Beware of the Pink Assassin (Your Tongue): The True Vine (Yashu'a, Jesus) Power of Life and Death is in the Tongue; Speaking God's (אלהים Elŏhíym) "Will" for Your Life into Existence!

CHILDREN OF THE MOST HIGH:
PRISTINE YOUTH AND FAMILY SOLUTIONS, LLC.
SONS AND DAUGHTERS OF THE MOST HIGH PUBLISHERS ®

Oh, Gracious Most High Heavenly father, Holy is your name, Your Will Be Done Now and Forever!

What are Idle Words, Idol Worship, Idolizing the Opposite of God, and Worshiping Idly? In the KJV bible book of Matthew chapter 12 verse 36; the Messiah Yashu'a (Jesus) said: "But I say unto you, that every idle (ἀργός Argos - (as a negative particle) inactive, (by implication) lazy, useless: barren, idle, slow) word (ῥῆμα Rhēma) that men (ἄνθρωπος Anthrōpos – people, human beings) shall speak, they shall give account thereof in the day of judgment. For by thy words thou shalt be justified, and by thy words thou shalt be condemned." In the KJV bible book of Exodus chapter 20 verse 4; it states: "Thou shalt not make unto thee any **graven image** (פֶּסֶל FEH-SEL, **Pecel** – means an **idol**:—carved (graven) image), or any likeness of anything that is in heaven above, or that is in the earth beneath, or that is in the water under the earth."

127

"And whatsoever we ask, we receive of him, because we keep his commandments, and do those things that are pleasing in his sight, KJV 1 John 3:22."

Beware of the Pink Assassin (Your Tongue): The True Vine
(Yashu'a, Jesus) Power of Life and Death is in the Tongue;
Speaking God's (אלהים Elôhîym) "Will"
for Your Life into Existence!

CHILDREN OF THE MOST HIGH:
PRISTINE YOUTH AND FAMILY SOLUTIONS, LLC.
SONS AND DAUGHTERS OF THE MOST HIGH PUBLISHERS ®

*Oh, Gracious Most High Heavenly father, Holy is your name,
Your Will Be Done Now and Forever!*

So, are pictures a sin? NO! This verse is referring to pro-creation of Adam and Eve who were made in the image and likeness of God (Genesis 1:26). After these new beings were procreated, no one was allowed to "**fashion**" anything in the likeness of that in the skies on earth or inside the earth. That's who the aforementioned quote was originally directed towards because we fell from grace after the fall in the Garden in Eden. So, Exodus 20:4 is in reference to **graven images and idols of worship**; not images of your relatives or even yourself (selfies), but the making of images in place of **God (אלהים Elôhîym)**. So, the concept that pictures of your relatives being a sin, or some form of **idol worship**; especially with marginalized people, is promoted by **the power of death in the tongue**. Pictures have the ability to **inspire positive memories and positive words in the minds and hearts of people that can speak True Vine (Yashu'a, Jesus) Power of Life into existence** by the "WILL" of the Most High **for our lives**!

128

"And whatsoever we ask, we receive of him, because we keep his commandments, and do those things that are pleasing in his sight, KJV 1 John 3:22."

Beware of the Pink Assassin (Your Tongue): The True Vine (Yashu'a, Jesus) Power of Life and Death is in the Tongue; Speaking God's (אלהים Elόhîym) "Will" for Your Life into Existence!

CHILDREN OF THE MOST HIGH:
PRISTINE YOUTH AND FAMILY SOLUTIONS, LLC.
SONS AND DAUGHTERS OF THE MOST HIGH PUBLISHERS ®

Oh, Gracious Most High Heavenly father, Holy is your name, Your Will Be Done Now and Forever!

According to the Online American Heritage Dictionary (2020), **idolizing** is defined as: "to regard with great or uncritical admiration or devotion. **To worship as an idol. Idly** is defined as: **Disinclined to work or be active; lazy. Lacking substance, value, or basis. To pass time without being engaged in purposeful activity.**" "The **effectual fervent prayer** (ἐνεργέω **Energeō – means: to be operative, be at work, put forth power to be active, efficient: —do**) of a righteous man [**human being**] availeth much, KJV James 5:16;" when speaking **the True Vine (Yashu'a, Jesus) Power of Life in the Tongue! You can teach a person how to pray, but; you can't make a person have faith in their own prayer!** "Love not the world, neither the things that are in the world. If any man [**human being**] loves the world, the love of the Father is not in him [**or her**]. For all that is in the world, the lust of the flesh, and the lust of the eyes, and the pride of life, is not of the Father, but is of the world. And the world passeth away, and the lust thereof: but he [**or she**] that doeth the will of God abideth forever, KJV 1st John 2:15-17." **Therefore, worshiping idly, and engaging in idolizing the opposite of God; leads to speaking death through the Power of the Tongue!**

129

"And whatsoever we ask, we receive of him, because we keep his commandments, and do those things that are pleasing in his sight, KJV 1 John 3:22."

Beware of the Pink Assassin (Your Tongue): The True Vine
(Yashu'a, Jesus) Power of Life and Death is in the Tongue;
Speaking God's (אלהים Elohîym) "Will"
for Your Life into Existence!

CHILDREN OF THE MOST HIGH:
PRISTINE YOUTH AND FAMILY SOLUTIONS, LLC.
SONS AND DAUGHTERS OF THE MOST HIGH PUBLISHERS ®

*Oh, Gracious Most High Heavenly father, Holy is your name,
Your Will Be Done Now and Forever!*

Please explain the Thayer's Greek Bible Lexicon (2011)
definition of "the Word (λόγος Logos)" being: the doctrine
concerning the attainment through Christ of salvation in
the kingdom of God? How can a person receive the holy
spirit? And is this a mandatory step to growing the habit of
speaking the True Vine (Yashu'a, Jesus) Power of Life
INTO EXISTENCE by the "Will" of the Most High
Heavenly Father for your life? A child of the Most High
must first become aware of what they value the most. If a
child of the Most High values spiritual growth aspiration,
according to the bible, a person must be born again. In the KJV
bible book of John chapter 3 verses 3-9; Yashu'a (Jesus) said:
"Verily, verily, I say unto thee, except a man **[person]** be
born again, he **[a person]** cannot see the kingdom of God."

130
"And whatsoever we ask, we receive of him,
because we keep his commandments, and do those
things that are pleasing in his sight, KJV 1 John 3:22."

Beware of the Pink Assassin (Your Tongue): The True Vine
(Yashu'a, Jesus) Power of Life and Death is in the Tongue;
**Speaking God's (אלהים Elohíym) "Will"
for Your Life into Existence!**

CHILDREN OF THE MOST HIGH:
PRISTINE YOUTH AND FAMILY SOLUTIONS, LLC.
SONS AND DAUGHTERS OF THE MOST HIGH PUBLISHERS ®

*Oh, Gracious Most High Heavenly father, Holy is your name,
Your Will Be Done Now and Forever!*

"Nicodemus saith unto him, how can a man **[person]** be born when he **[a person]** is old? can he **[a person]** enter the second time into his mother's womb, and be born? Yashu'a said: "Verily, verily, I say unto thee, except a man **[person]** be born of water and of the Spirit, **[a person]** cannot enter into the kingdom of God. That which is born of the flesh is flesh; and that which is born of the Spirit is spirit. Marvel not that I said unto thee, Ye must be born again. The wind bloweth where it listeth, and thou hearest the sound thereof, but canst not tell whence it cometh, and whither it goeth: so is every one that is born of the Spirit."

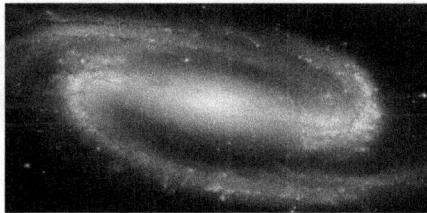

131

**"And whatsoever we ask, we receive of him,
because we keep his commandments, and do those
things that are pleasing in his sight, KJV 1 John 3:22."**

Beware of the Pink Assassin (Your Tongue): The True Vine (Yashu'a, Jesus) Power of Life and Death is in the Tongue; Speaking God's (אלהים Elohîym) "Will" for Your Life into Existence!

CHILDREN OF THE MOST HIGH:
PRISTINE YOUTH AND FAMILY SOLUTIONS, LLC.
SONS AND DAUGHTERS OF THE MOST HIGH PUBLISHERS ®

Oh, Gracious Most High Heavenly father, Holy is your name, Your Will Be Done Now and Forever!

In the KJV bible book of Romans chapter 10 verses 9-10; it states: "That if thou shalt confess with thy mouth the Lord Jesus, and shalt believe in thine heart that God hath raised him from the dead, thou shalt be saved. For with the heart **[of a person]** believeth unto righteousness; and with the mouth confession is made unto salvation." Receiving the holy spirit is a mandatory step to **Developing the Habit the True Vine (Yashu'a, Jesus) Power of Life and Death in the Tongue, being SPOKEN INTO EXISTENCE by the "Will" of the Most High Heavenly Father for your life!**

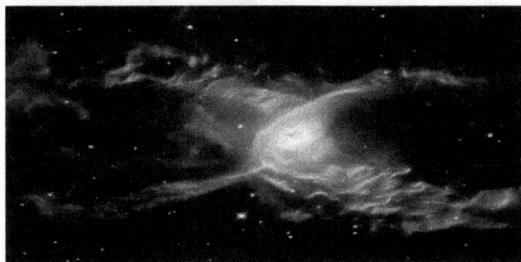

132

"And whatsoever we ask, we receive of him, because we keep his commandments, and do those things that are pleasing in his sight, KJV 1 John 3:22."

Beware of the Pink Assassin (Your Tongue): The True Vine (Yashu'a, Jesus) Power of Life and Death is in the Tongue; Speaking God's (אלהים Elŏhîym) "Will" for Your Life into Existence!

CHILDREN OF THE MOST HIGH:
PRISTINE YOUTH AND FAMILY SOLUTIONS, LLC.
SONS AND DAUGHTERS OF THE MOST HIGH PUBLISHERS ®

Oh, Gracious Most High Heavenly father, Holy is your name,
Your Will Be Done Now and Forever!

The aforementioned verses gives' a person some insight into being born again. However, there is a plethora of additional lifelong works that a person has to do on themselves as they grow spiritually. Meaning, you have to rid yourself of everything that you think is right so that the holy spirit can access your temple (body). In the KJV bible book of 1st Corinthians chapter 6 verses 19-20; it states: "What? know ye not that your body is the temple of the Holy Ghost which is in you, which ye have of God, and ye are not your own? For ye are bought with a price: therefore, glorify God in your body, and in your spirit, which are God's." In the KJV bible book of 1st Corinthians chapter 3 verses 16-17; it states: "Know ye not that ye are the temple of God, and that the Spirit of God dwelleth in you? If any [person] defile the temple of God, [that person] shall God destroy; for the temple of God is holy, which temple ye are."

133

"And whatsoever we ask, we receive of him, because we keep his commandments, and do those things that are pleasing in his sight, KJV 1 John 3:22."

Beware of the Pink Assassin (Your Tongue): The True Vine
(Yashu'a, Jesus) Power of Life and Death is in the Tongue;
Speaking God's (אלהים Elòhîym) "Will"
for Your Life into Existence!

CHILDREN OF THE MOST HIGH:
PRISTINE YOUTH AND FAMILY SOLUTIONS, LLC.
SONS AND DAUGHTERS OF THE MOST HIGH PUBLISHERS ®

*Oh, Gracious Most High Heavenly father, Holy is your name,
Your Will Be Done Now and Forever!*

So, the holy spirit can only come into a clean temple (body).
The holy spirit can only stay in a comfortable, purified temple
(body). This means, a person who is contemplating rather or not
they are ready to receive the holy spirit has to be willing to
commit themselves to moment to moment work of eradicating
negative habits, negative thinking, negative speaking, negative
intentions, negative aspirations, negative actions, and unhealthy
eating. If a person does not eradicate themselves of the above-
mentioned negative attributes, **a holy (pure) spirit (Pneuma,
Greek), Nephesh (Aramic/Hebrew) cannot dwell inside an
impure mind, impure heart and impure body. Developing
the Habit of the True Vine (Yashu'a, Jesus) Power of Life
and Death in the Tongue, being SPOKEN INTO
EXISTENCE by the "Will" of the Most High Heavenly
Father for your life**, requires active discipline exhibited
moment to moment on a daily basis. It is a serious commitment
of **discipline** that is required in order to keep your temple
(body) purified mentally, spiritually, emotionally and
physically.

134
**"And whatsoever we ask, we receive of him,
because we keep his commandments, and do those
things that are pleasing in his sight, KJV 1 John 3:22."**

Beware of the Pink Assassin (Your Tongue): The True Vine
(Yashu'a, Jesus) Power of Life and Death is in the Tongue;
Speaking God's (אלהים Elŏhîym) "Will"
for Your Life into Existence!

CHILDREN OF THE MOST HIGH:
PRISTINE YOUTH AND FAMILY SOLUTIONS, LLC.
SONS AND DAUGHTERS OF THE MOST HIGH PUBLISHERS ®

*Oh, Gracious Most High Heavenly father, Holy is your name,
Your Will Be Done Now and Forever!*

The Online American Heritage Dictionary (2020) defines
discipline as:

**"1. Training expected to produce a specific character or
pattern of behavior, especially training that produces moral
or mental improvement: was raised in the strictest
discipline.**

**2. b. Controlled behavior resulting from disciplinary
training; self-control."**

The Children of the Most High Pristine Youth and Family
Solutions, LLC. defines **discipline** as: **"doing what you need
to do when it needs to be done whether you feel like doing it
or not."** Some people may make the mistake of thinking that
they can just cleanse their mind and spirit without cleansing
their body (temple) from unhealthy eating and unhealthy
drinking.

135

**"And whatsoever we ask, we receive of him,
because we keep his commandments, and do those
things that are pleasing in his sight, KJV 1 John 3:22."**

Beware of the Pink Assassin (Your Tongue): The True Vine
(Yashu'a, Jesus) Power of Life and Death is in the Tongue;
Speaking God's (אלהים Elŏhîym) "Will"
for Your Life into Existence!

CHILDREN OF THE MOST HIGH:
PRISTINE YOUTH AND FAMILY SOLUTIONS, LLC.
SONS AND DAUGHTERS OF THE MOST HIGH PUBLISHERS ®

*Oh, Gracious Most High Heavenly father, Holy is your name,
Your Will Be Done Now and Forever!*

Many people may make statements like: **"In my heart, I'm
good and that's all that matters." "As long as I have God in
my heart, that's all that matters."** <u>**If that were the case, the
Most High would put the truth in our hearts instead of in
books and scriptures**</u>.

136

**"And whatsoever we ask, we receive of him,
because we keep his commandments, and do those
things that are pleasing in his sight, KJV 1 John 3:22."**

Beware of the Pink Assassin (Your Tongue): The True Vine (Yashu'a, Jesus) Power of Life and Death is in the Tongue; Speaking God's (אלהים Elŏhíym) "Will" for Your Life into Existence!

CHILDREN OF THE MOST HIGH:
PRISTINE YOUTH AND FAMILY SOLUTIONS, LLC.
SONS AND DAUGHTERS OF THE MOST HIGH PUBLISHERS ®

Oh, Gracious Most High Heavenly father, Holy is your name,
Your Will Be Done Now and Forever!

Why would the Most High put the truth in a book like the Torah, Bible or other scriptures or a book like the one you are reading right now, when the Most High could have just put the information in our hearts?

Because there is a part of **developing the habit of speaking the True Vine (Yashu'a, Jesus) Power of Life INTO EXISTENCE by the "Will" of the Most High Heavenly Father <u>for your life</u>** that is verbal and physical, that requires great discipline in order to not give into **the temptations of the 9 Deadly Venoms of the Desires of the dragon, that old serpent called the devil and satan that deceived the whole world.** The great discipline to not give into the temptations of the 9 Deadly Venoms is essential to overall potential spiritual growth success because the temptations cannot work on the soul, they can only work on the body.

137

"And whatsoever we ask, we receive of him, because we keep his commandments, and do those things that are pleasing in his sight, KJV 1 John 3:22."

Beware of the Pink Assassin (Your Tongue): The True Vine (Yashu'a, Jesus) Power of Life and Death is in the Tongue; Speaking God's (אלהים Elohîym) "Will" for Your Life into Existence!

CHILDREN OF THE MOST HIGH:
PRISTINE YOUTH AND FAMILY SOLUTIONS, LLC.
SONS AND DAUGHTERS OF THE MOST HIGH PUBLISHERS ®

Oh, Gracious Most High Heavenly father, Holy is your name, Your Will Be Done Now and Forever!

The body interprets the temptations for the soul. **For example:** As it relates to lusts, sometimes, the temptation is put on television through images of nudity in effort **to plant the thought in the mind** for the soul to interpret as lusts. So, when a person receives the holy spirit, he or she transforms from a son or daughter of human beings to a child of the Most High and the holy spirit will reeducate your soul over time and substantiate what you learn as the Most High's truth through evidence, reasoning and experience. Essentially, a person would have to make what the Children of the Most High: Pristine Youth and Family Solutions, LLC. refer to as a: "**True Vine "Yashu'a (Jesus) Conscious and Conscientious (C.A.C.) decision**" that will allow their mind to develop **the habit of speaking the True Vine (Yashu'a, Jesus) Power of Life INTO EXISTENCE by the "Will" of the Most High Heavenly Father <u>for your life</u>**.

138

"And whatsoever we ask, we receive of him, because we keep his commandments, and do those things that are pleasing in his sight, KJV 1 John 3:22."

Beware of the Pink Assassin (Your Tongue): The True Vine
(Yashu'a, Jesus) Power of Life and Death is in the Tongue;
Speaking God's (אלהים Elŏhîym) "Will"
for Your Life into Existence!

CHILDREN OF THE MOST HIGH:
PRISTINE YOUTH AND FAMILY SOLUTIONS, LLC.
SONS AND DAUGHTERS OF THE MOST HIGH PUBLISHERS ®

Oh, Gracious Most High Heavenly father, Holy is your name,
Your Will Be Done Now and Forever!

This decision process is also referred to by the Children of the
Most High: Pristine Youth and Family Solutions, LLC. as:
**"Choices, Actions, Consequences and Repercussions
(C.A.C.A.R) through Potential Diversification and
Overstanding**." Dr. Leah refers to this process as: "The Brain
Does the Bidding of the Mind, Leah, 2013, p.32)."

What is Potential Diversification? According to the Children
of the Most High: Pristine Youth and Family Solutions, LLC.,
"**Potential Diversification** is having or showing the capacity to
create a number of different concepts into something positive
that will benefit you and others in the present and in the future.
Potential Diversification is also having the ability to utilize
your mental capacity to develop resources and use them more
efficiently or to reduce risks that may not lead to positive
outcomes in your life, (Hughes, 2019)."

139

**"And whatsoever we ask, we receive of him,
because we keep his commandments, and do those
things that are pleasing in his sight, KJV 1 John 3:22."**

Beware of the Pink Assassin (Your Tongue): The True Vine
(Yashu'a, Jesus) Power of Life and Death is in the Tongue;
Speaking God's (אלהים Eloȟîym) "Will"
for Your Life into Existence!

CHILDREN OF THE MOST HIGH:
PRISTINE YOUTH AND FAMILY SOLUTIONS, LLC.
SONS AND DAUGHTERS OF THE MOST HIGH PUBLISHERS ⚜

*Oh, Gracious Most High Heavenly father, Holy is your name,
Your Will Be Done Now and Forever!*

What does the words: "Overstanding and Overstand" mean to the Children of the Most High: Pristine Youth and Family Solutions, LLC.? "Overstanding is mastering the comprehension of what is understood or what many may not have an understanding of."

Therefore, the Children of the Most High: Pristine Youth and Family Solution, LLC. define the word: "**Overstand**" as: <u>having the ability by way of the Most High Heavenly Father to master the ability to clearly teach and explain the Most High's Scriptural knowledge from the original languages that the scriptures were revealed in; inclusive of teaching the children of the Most High how to study and research the Most High's scriptures in the original languages that they were revealed through the principles that the acronym "S.E.R.V.E." represent</u>, Hughes, 2019."

140
"And whatsoever we ask, we receive of him, because we keep his commandments, and do those things that are pleasing in his sight, KJV 1 John 3:22."

Beware of the Pink Assassin (Your Tongue): The True Vine (Yashu'a, Jesus) Power of Life and Death is in the Tongue; Speaking God's (אלהים Elôhîym) "Will" for Your Life into Existence!

CHILDREN OF THE MOST HIGH:
PRISTINE YOUTH AND FAMILY SOLUTIONS, LLC.
SONS AND DAUGHTERS OF THE MOST HIGH PUBLISHERS ®

Oh, Gracious Most High Heavenly father, Holy is your name, Your Will Be Done Now and Forever!

What do the acronyms of: S.E.R.V.E. represent to the Children of the Most High; Pristine Youth and Family Solution, LLC.?

The acronyms of: **S.E.R.V.E.** represents: **S**erving, **E**ducation, **R**esearching, **V**olunteering, and **E**ntrepreneurship. So, the values of serving and volunteering, the process of receiving instruction through the reversal of mis-education, and the acquisition of God's **(אלהים Elôhîym)** evidence-based **A.W.A.R.E. (All Wise Abundant Right Exact)** knowledge. This occurs through novice, non-bias life-long researching. Also, the benefits of entrepreneurship education are instilled in youth and adult participants who learn and practice the potent 9x9 True Vine (Yashu'a, Jesus) B.A.-K.A.-R.E. Sequential Order of Learning God's **(אלהים Elôhîym)** evidence-based **A.W.A.R.E. (All Wise Abundant Right Exact)** knowledge, (Hughes, 2019).

141

"And whatsoever we ask, we receive of him, because we keep his commandments, and do those things that are pleasing in his sight, KJV 1 John 3:22."

Beware of the Pink Assassin (Your Tongue): The True Vine
(Yashu'a, Jesus) Power of Life and Death is in the Tongue;
Speaking God's (אלהים Elŏhîym) "Will"
for Your Life into Existence!

CHILDREN OF THE MOST HIGH:
PRISTINE YOUTH AND FAMILY SOLUTIONS, LLC.
SONS AND DAUGHTERS OF THE MOST HIGH PUBLISHERS ®

Oh, Gracious Most High Heavenly father, Holy is your name,
Your Will Be Done Now and Forever!

Define the word "education". According to Craft (1984), he
noted that there are two different Latin roots of the English
word "**education.**" They are "**educare,**" which means to train
or to mold, and "**educere,**" meaning to lead out or bring out.
While the two meanings are quite different, they are both
represented in the word "**education.**" To educate' comes from
'educere': 'to bring out/draw out'. According to the Online
American Heritage Dictionary (2020), education is: "The act or
process of educating or being educated. The knowledge or skill
obtained or developed by a learning process. A program of
instruction of a specified kind or level: *driver education; a*
college education. The field of study that is concerned with the
pedagogy of teaching and learning. An instructive or
enlightening experience: *Her work in an animal shelter was a*
real education."

142

"And whatsoever we ask, we receive of him,
because we keep his commandments, and do those
things that are pleasing in his sight, KJV 1 John 3:22."

Beware of the Pink Assassin (Your Tongue): The True Vine (Yashu'a, Jesus) Power of Life and Death is in the Tongue; Speaking God's (אלהים Elŏhîym) "Will" for Your Life into Existence!

CHILDREN OF THE MOST HIGH:
PRISTINE YOUTH AND FAMILY SOLUTIONS, LLC.
SONS AND DAUGHTERS OF THE MOST HIGH PUBLISHERS ®

Oh, Gracious Most High Heavenly father, Holy is your name, Your Will Be Done Now and Forever!

How does Wickedness utilize the Power of the Tongue to deceive and influence what some people think and feel?

According to the KJV bible book of Psalms chapter 58 verses 3-5; <u>wicked people are born wicked</u> and as soon as they can **talk**, they **speak** lies. Their <u>lying tongues</u> **charm, deceive** and **influence** what some people think and feel; they are of their father the devil. "The **wicked** are estranged <u>from the womb</u>: **they go astray as soon as they <u>be born</u>** (בֶּטֶן Beten which means: **to be born, as seat of mental faculties, as they be born, within, womb**), <u>speaking lies</u>. Their poison is like the poison of a serpent: they are like the deaf adder that stoppeth her ear. Which will not hearken to the voice of charmers, charming never so wisely, KJV Psalms 58:3-5."

143

"And whatsoever we ask, we receive of him, because we keep his commandments, and do those things that are pleasing in his sight, KJV 1 John 3:22."

Beware of the Pink Assassin (Your Tongue): The True Vine (Yashu'a, Jesus) Power of Life and Death is in the Tongue; Speaking God's (אלהים Elohîym) "Will" for Your Life into Existence!

CHILDREN OF THE MOST HIGH:
PRISTINE YOUTH AND FAMILY SOLUTIONS, LLC.
SONS AND DAUGHTERS OF THE MOST HIGH PUBLISHERS ®

Oh, Gracious Most High Heavenly father, Holy is your name, Your Will Be Done Now and Forever!

When confronted by the **wicked people**, the Messiah Yashu'a (Jesus) **said**: "Ye are of your father the devil, and the lusts of your father ye will do. He was a murderer from the beginning, and abode not in the truth, because there is no truth in him. When he speaketh a lie, he speaketh of his own: for he is a liar, and the father of it, KJV John 8:44." "These six things **doth the LORD hate**: yea, seven are an abomination unto him: A proud look, **a lying tongue**, and hands that shed innocent blood, an **a heart that deviseth wicked imaginations**, feet that be swift in running to mischief, a false witness that **speaketh lies**, and **he that soweth discord among brethren** [**through their words**], KJV Proverbs 6:16-19." So, according to the aforementioned, **wickedness utilizes the Power of the Tongue to deceive and influence what some people think and feel by charming them through speaking lies!**

144

"And whatsoever we ask, we receive of him, because we keep his commandments, and do those things that are pleasing in his sight, KJV 1 John 3:22."

Beware of the Pink Assassin (Your Tongue): The True Vine
(Yashu'a, Jesus) Power of Life and Death is in the Tongue;
**Speaking God's (אלהים Elóhîym) "Will"
for Your Life into Existence!**

CHILDREN OF THE MOST HIGH:
PRISTINE YOUTH AND FAMILY SOLUTIONS, LLC.
SONS AND DAUGHTERS OF THE MOST HIGH PUBLISHERS ®

*Oh, Gracious Most High Heavenly father, Holy is your name,
Your Will Be Done Now and Forever!*

In the KJV bible book of John chapter 7 verse 16; the Messiah
Yashu'a (Jesus) said: "My doctrine is not mine, but his that
sent me." "**My doctrine** shall drop as the rain, my speech shall
distil as the dew, as the small rain upon the tender herb, and as
the showers upon the grass, KJV Deuteronomy 32:2." "For thou
hast said, **My doctrine** is pure, and I am clean in thine eyes,
KJV Job 11:4." "But thou hast fully known my doctrine,
manner of life, purpose, faith, longsuffering, charity, patience,
KJV 2 Timothy 3:10." "For I give you good doctrine, forsake
ye not my law, KJV Proverbs 4:2." So, the **Doctrine of the
Most High is above ALL-Demon-Nations, and is above
ALL-Denom-i-Nations. The Doctrine of the Most High is
the Pure! God's (אלהים Elôhîym) A.W.A.R.E. (All Wise,
And Right Exact) Knowledge is essential to Becoming
Aware (B.A.) of the Knowledge that must be Applied (K.A.),
that at a later stage of one's positive mental, spiritual,
emotional, and physical growth; the children of the Most
High Reflect on their Experiences (R.E.).**

145

**"And whatsoever we ask, we receive of him,
because we keep his commandments, and do those
things that are pleasing in his sight, KJV 1 John 3:22."**

Beware of the Pink Assassin (Your Tongue): The True Vine
(Yashu'a, Jesus) Power of Life and Death is in the Tongue;
Speaking God's (אלהים Elŏhîym) "Will"
for Your Life into Existence!

CHILDREN OF THE MOST HIGH:
PRISTINE YOUTH AND FAMILY SOLUTIONS, LLC.
SONS AND DAUGHTERS OF THE MOST HIGH PUBLISHERS ®

*Oh, Gracious Most High Heavenly father, Holy is your name,
Your Will Be Done Now and Forever!*

The Doctrine of the Most High is the Life in the Power in the Tongue Spoken Words that the Messiah (Yashu'a, Jesus) Taught! "But speaking the truth in love, may grow up into him in all things, which is the head, even Christ, KJV Ephesians 4:15." So, by **Speaking** the **True-Vine (Yashu'a, Jesus) Truth through the Power of the Tongue to Kills Negative Habits!** Therefore; the children of the Most High must continuously put the following words in A.C.T.I.O.N. (Activated, Conscious, Timely, Intentions, Obligated, Now) through all of our works, and in all that we are graciously blessed with the opportunity to do: "On my own accord, I can of mine own self do nothing, I seek not mine own will, but the will of the Father which hath sent me" according to the Most High Heavenly Father's pre**ordained purpose** for your life." **Mind Gardening in the Creative Garden of Will (Your Mind) to grow the habit of speaking the True Vine (Yashu'a, Jesus) Power of Life INTO EXISTENCE by the "Will" of the Most High Heavenly Father for your life!**

146
**"And whatsoever we ask, we receive of him,
because we keep his commandments, and do those
things that are pleasing in his sight, KJV 1 John 3:22."**

CHILDREN OF THE MOST HIGH:
PRISTINE YOUTH AND FAMILY SOLUTIONS, LLC.
SONS AND DAUGHTERS OF THE MOST HIGH PUBLISHERS *

Oh, Gracious Most High Heavenly father, Holy is your name, Your Will Be Done Now and Forever!

Chapter 7: I AM THAT I AM!
Open your Heart before Opening your Mouth; and Always Remember that Words Should Be Soft, not Hard!

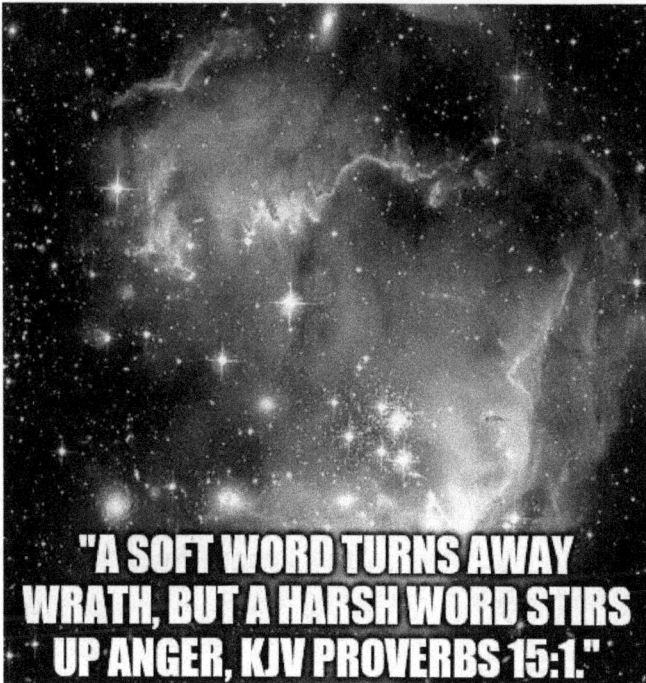

"A SOFT WORD TURNS AWAY WRATH, BUT A HARSH WORD STIRS UP ANGER, KJV PROVERBS 15:1."

147

"And whatsoever we ask, we receive of him, because we keep his commandments, and do those things that are pleasing in his sight, KJV 1 John 3:22."

CHILDREN OF THE MOST HIGH:
PRISTINE YOUTH AND FAMILY SOLUTIONS, LLC.
SONS AND DAUGHTERS OF THE MOST HIGH PUBLISHERS ®

*Oh, Gracious Most High Heavenly father, Holy is your name,
Your Will Be Done Now and Forever!*

In this chapter, we will utilize the Online KJV bible Greek Strong's Concordance (2020), "**the Word** (λόγος **Logos**) definitions of: **a word, uttered by a living voice, embodies a conception or idea, the Divine Expression (Christ), the mind alone, mental faculty of thinking, the divine mind, Declaration of Faith**." "**Nothing Would Exist if the Most High didn't Create It**," "**Hear, O Israel: The LORD our God is one LORD**," and "**In the beginning was the Word, and the Word was with God, and the Word was God**," are all examples of "**the Word** (λόγος **Logos**) as a **Declaration of Faith**. This declaration, or statement of faith, in **Ashuric/Syriac Arabic** is called الكلمة "**Al Kalima**," which literally means "**The Word**". So, **the Word** (λόγος **Logos**) as a **Declaration of Faith** is an example of how the **True Vine (Yashu'a, Jesus), Power of the Tongue Speaks Life INTO EXISTENCE by the "Will" of the Most High Heavenly Father <u>for your life</u>**!

148

"And whatsoever we ask, we receive of him, because we keep his commandments, and do those things that are pleasing in his sight, KJV 1 John 3:22."

Beware of the Pink Assassin (Your Tongue): The True Vine
(Yashu'a, Jesus) Power of Life and Death is in the Tongue;
Speaking God's (אלהים Elơhîym) "Will"
for Your Life into Existence!

CHILDREN OF THE MOST HIGH:
PRISTINE YOUTH AND FAMILY SOLUTIONS, LLC.
SONS AND DAUGHTERS OF THE MOST HIGH PUBLISHERS ®

*Oh, Gracious Most High Heavenly father, Holy is your name,
Your Will Be Done Now and Forever!*

Is Character Assassination an example of how the Power of the Tongue can Speak Death into existence?

According to the Online American Heritage Dictionary (2020), it defines: character assassination as the malicious denunciation or slandering of another person, especially as part of an effort to ruin the reputation of a public figure." So, **character assassination occurs through the utilization malicious denunciation or slandering of <u>written</u> and <u>spoken</u> WORDS**! Therefore, **Character Assassination is an example of how the Power of the Tongue can Speak Death into existence.**

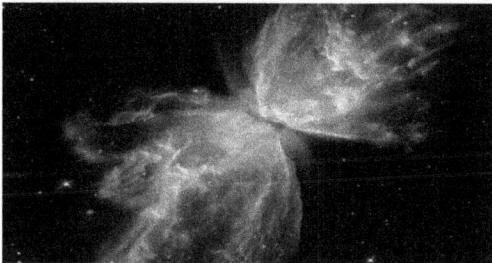

149

**"And whatsoever we ask, we receive of him,
because we keep his commandments, and do those
things that are pleasing in his sight, KJV 1 John 3:22."**

Beware of the Pink Assassin (Your Tongue): The True Vine
(Yashu'a, Jesus) Power of Life and Death is in the Tongue;
Speaking God's (אלהים Eloĥîym) "Will"
for Your Life into Existence!

CHILDREN OF THE MOST HIGH:
PRISTINE YOUTH AND FAMILY SOLUTIONS, LLC.
SONS AND DAUGHTERS OF THE MOST HIGH PUBLISHERS ®

*Oh, Gracious Most High Heavenly father, Holy is your name,
Your Will Be Done Now and Forever!*

Does the Word (λόγος Logos) definitions of: **The Divine
Expression (Christ), the mind alone, mental faculty of
thinking, the divine mind, also personify as Spirit?** In the
aforementioned KJV Blue Letter bible Greek Strong's
Concordance (2020), thorough explanation of the KJV bible
book John chapter 1 verse 1; when it says: "**In the beginning
(ἀρχή Archē) was the word for (Word):** λόγος Logos, defined
as: **reasoning (the mental faculty), the Divine Expression
(Christ), of speech, a word uttered by a living voice, the
MIND alone**, reason, **the mental faculty of thinking;**" is there
a correlation with the Messiah being before Abraham, and
Genesis chapter 1 verses 1 and 2?**

150

**"And whatsoever we ask, we receive of him,
because we keep his commandments, and do those
things that are pleasing in his sight, KJV 1 John 3:22."**

Beware of the Pink Assassin (Your Tongue): The True Vine
(Yashu'a, Jesus) Power of Life and Death is in the Tongue;
Speaking God's (אלהים Elóhîym) "Will"
for Your Life into Existence!

CHILDREN OF THE MOST HIGH:
PRISTINE YOUTH AND FAMILY SOLUTIONS, LLC.
SONS AND DAUGHTERS OF THE MOST HIGH PUBLISHERS ®

*Oh, Gracious Most High Heavenly father, Holy is your name,
Your Will Be Done Now and Forever!*

In the KJV bible book of John chapter 8 verse 58, **the Messiah Yashu'a (Jesus)** said: "Verily (ἀμήν **Amēn**), verily (ἀμήν **Amēn**), I say unto you, Before Abraham was, I (ἐγώ **Egō**)." Am (εἰμί **Eimi** pronounced as: **A-me'(I Me).**" How did **the Messiah Yashu'a (Jesus) exist in the beginning** (ἀρχή **Archē** pronounced as **Ar-Khay') of the KJV bible if he was not born until sometime in the New Testament?** According to the KJV bible book of John chapter 1 verse 14, and Matthew chapter 2 verse 1; where it states: "And **the Word was made flesh** (σάρξ **Sarx** – pronounced as: **Sä'rks** and means: **human flesh (the soft substance of the living body, which covers the bones and is permeated with blood, the body of a man)**, and dwelt among us, (and we beheld his glory, the glory as of the only begotten of the Father,) full of grace and truth."

151

"And whatsoever we ask, we receive of him, because we keep his commandments, and do those things that are pleasing in his sight, KJV 1 John 3:22."

Beware of the Pink Assassin (Your Tongue): The True Vine
(Yashu'a, Jesus) Power of Life and Death is in the Tongue;
Speaking God's (אלהים Elo'hîym) "Will"
for Your Life into Existence!

CHILDREN OF THE MOST HIGH:
PRISTINE YOUTH AND FAMILY SOLUTIONS, LLC.
SONS AND DAUGHTERS OF THE MOST HIGH PUBLISHERS ®

*Oh, Gracious Most High Heavenly father, Holy is your name,
Your Will Be Done Now and Forever!*

"Now when Jesus was born in **Bethlehem** (Βηθλέεμ **Bēthleem**
– pronounced as: **Ba-thle'-em**) and means: "**House of Bread**"
The Messiah Yashu'a (Jesus) said that: "I AM the Living
Bread)" of Judaea in the days of Herod the king, behold, there
came wise men from the east to Jerusalem." In the KJV bible
book of John chapter 6 verse 51; the Messiah Yashu'a (Jesus)
said: "I am the living bread which came down from heaven:
if any man (τις **Tis – which means a male or female person**)
eat of this bread, he [**or she**] shall live forever: and the bread
that I will give is my flesh, which I will give for the life of the
world."

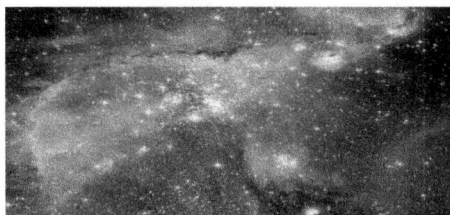

152

**"And whatsoever we ask, we receive of him,
because we keep his commandments, and do those
things that are pleasing in his sight, KJV 1 John 3:22."**

Beware of the Pink Assassin (Your Tongue): The True Vine
(Yashu'a, Jesus) Power of Life and Death is in the Tongue;
Speaking God's (אלהים Elóhîym) "Will"
for Your Life into Existence!

CHILDREN OF THE MOST HIGH:
PRISTINE YOUTH AND FAMILY SOLUTIONS, LLC.
SONS AND DAUGHTERS OF THE MOST HIGH PUBLISHERS ®

Oh, Gracious Most High Heavenly father, Holy is your name,
Your Will Be Done Now and Forever!

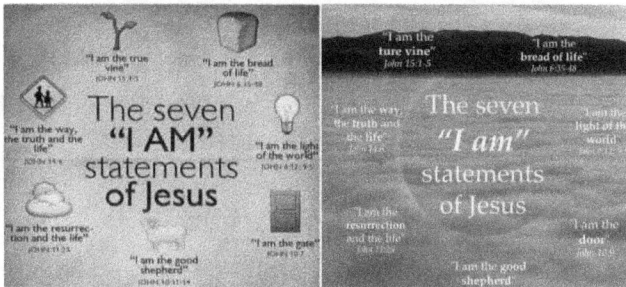

In the Online KJV Blue Letter bible Greek Strong's
Concordance (2020), all of the Yashu'a (Jesus), "I AM"
statements utilize the same phrase: I (ἐγώ Egō)." Am (εἰμί
Eimi pronounced as: **A-me'(I Me)."** In the KJV bible book of
Exodus chapter 3 verse 14; it states: "And God said unto Moses,
I AM (הָיָה **Yahayyu, or Hayah** which means, **Existing One,
to be, to exist, be in existence**). **THAT I AM**: and he said,
Thus, shalt thou say unto the children of Israel, **I AM** (הָיָה
Yahayyu, or Hayah which means, **Existing One, to be to
exist, be in existence**) hath sent me unto you."

153

**"And whatsoever we ask, we receive of him,
because we keep his commandments, and do those
things that are pleasing in his sight, KJV 1 John 3:22."**

Beware of the Pink Assassin (Your Tongue): The True Vine
(Yashu'a, Jesus) Power of Life and Death is in the Tongue;
Speaking God's (אלהים Elohîym) "Will"
for Your Life into Existence!

CHILDREN OF THE MOST HIGH:
PRISTINE YOUTH AND FAMILY SOLUTIONS, LLC.
SONS AND DAUGHTERS OF THE MOST HIGH PUBLISHERS ®

Oh, Gracious Most High Heavenly father, Holy is your name,
Your Will Be Done Now and Forever!

So, as it relates to the **True Vine (Yashu'a, Jesus) Life being
in the Power of the Tongue**; the Children of the Most High,
Pristine Youth and Family Solutions, LLC., acknowledges **the
Real Messiah Jesus as our Savior** who **we refer to** in his
**original Galilean/Judean Aramic (Hebrew) language,
original birth name** Yasu'a (يسوع) or **Yashu'a** (ישרע)
meaning "**Savior**" also spelled **Yeshua** or **Yehoshu'a, Iesous**
(Ἰησοῦς) in the Greek translation and as **Kurios** (Greek word
for Lord), and **Issa** or **Isa** in Ashuric Syriac (Arabic). Now
when **Yehoshu'a** is translated in the Hebrew language it
translates as **Yahayyu Saves** or simply **Joshua**, and in the
Galilean language as Yashu'a or **Yasu'a** Inar **Rab** (which
translates as **Jesus Son of the Sustainer**), **Yashu'a Bar
Yahayyu** (باحب, **Existing One**).

154
**"And whatsoever we ask, we receive of him,
because we keep his commandments, and do those
things that are pleasing in his sight, KJV 1 John 3:22."**

Beware of the Pink Assassin (Your Tongue): The True Vine (Yashu'a, Jesus) Power of Life and Death is in the Tongue; Speaking God's (אלהים Elŏhîym) "Will" for Your Life into Existence!

CHILDREN OF THE MOST HIGH:
PRISTINE YOUTH AND FAMILY SOLUTIONS, LLC.
SONS AND DAUGHTERS OF THE MOST HIGH PUBLISHERS ®

*Oh, Gracious Most High Heavenly father, Holy is your name,
Your Will Be Done Now and Forever!*

In Modern Hebrew translates as **Savior Son of the Everliving** or **Savior Son of the Existing One** or **Living One**, **Yasu'** and **Haru** as **Karast "Christ"** to the **Ancient** original indigenous Egyptian people of what is called: "Egypt" today, not to be confused with the Egyptians who are the nonindigenous people who migrated to what is now known as Egypt. Yashu'a called **Jesus,** is **the Son of God** in English. **Yashu'a (Jesus), the Son of the Most High God** is the way back to the Most High! In the KJV bible book of Genesis chapter 1 verses 1-2 states: "**In the beginning** God created the heaven and the earth. And the earth was without form, and void; and darkness was upon the face of the deep. And **the Spirit of God** moved upon the face of the waters." The KJV bible book of John chapter 1 verses 1-3 states: "**In the beginning** was **the Word**, and **the Word** was **with God**, **and the Word was God**."

"And whatsoever we ask, we receive of him, because we keep his commandments, and do those things that are pleasing in his sight, KJV 1 John 3:22."

Beware of the Pink Assassin (Your Tongue): The True Vine
(Yashu'a, Jesus) Power of Life and Death is in the Tongue;
Speaking God's (אלהים Elốhîym) "Will"
for Your Life into Existence!

CHILDREN OF THE MOST HIGH:
PRISTINE YOUTH AND FAMILY SOLUTIONS, LLC.
SONS AND DAUGHTERS OF THE MOST HIGH PUBLISHERS ®

Oh, Gracious Most High Heavenly father, Holy is your name,
Your Will Be Done Now and Forever!

"<u>**The same was in the beginning with God**</u>. <u>**All things were**</u>
<u>**made by him; and without him was not anything made that**</u>
<u>**was made**</u>." So, the Messiah Yashu'a (Jesus) was <u>**in the**</u>
<u>**beginning**</u> <u>**as one with God or one with ALL**</u> in Genesis
chapter 1 before Abraham. The Messiah Yashu'a (Jesus) also
exists before Abraham as the <u>**Spirit of God**</u> <u>**that moved upon**</u>
<u>**the face of the waters**</u> in Genesis chapter 1 verse 2. When God
(אלהים **Elôhîym**) sends "<u>**the Spirit of God**</u>" to earth, <u>**the word**</u>
<u>**and the spirit**</u> became flesh as the Messiah Yashu'a (Jesus)
in the New Testament of the bible. The Most High Heavenly
Father's <u>**thought**</u> of "<u>**the Word**</u>," came **INTO EXISTENCE,**
and "<u>**the Word became flesh**</u>," **by the "Will" of the Most**
High Heavenly Father. "And <u>**the LORD said**</u>, <u>**My spirit**</u> shall
not always strive <u>**with man**</u> (<u>**a human being, singular**</u>), **for**
that he also <u>**is flesh**</u>: yet his days shall be a hundred and twenty
years, KJV Genesis 6:3."

156
"And whatsoever we ask, we receive of him,
because we keep his commandments, and do those
things that are pleasing in his sight, KJV 1 John 3:22."

Beware of the Pink Assassin (Your Tongue): The True Vine
(Yashu'a, Jesus) Power of Life and Death is in the Tongue;
Speaking God's (אלהים Elohíym) "Will"
for Your Life into Existence!

Oh, Gracious Most High Heavenly father, Holy is your name,
Your Will Be Done Now and Forever!

So, in the flesh of the physical body of the Messiah Yashu'a
(Jesus), the **Finite Christ-Mind** existed in spirit as one with the
Living Infinite Mind of the Most High Heavenly Father's as
the **thought** of "**the Word**," that came **INTO EXISTENCE,**
and "**the Word became flesh**," by the "Will" of the Most
High Heavenly Father as **infinite Mind of ALL**!

157

"And whatsoever we ask, we receive of him,
because we keep his commandments, and do those
things that are pleasing in his sight, KJV 1 John 3:22."

Beware of the Pink Assassin (Your Tongue): The True Vine (Yashu'a, Jesus) Power of Life and Death is in the Tongue; Speaking God's (אלהים Elóhîym) "Will" for Your Life into Existence!

CHILDREN OF THE MOST HIGH:
PRISTINE YOUTH AND FAMILY SOLUTIONS, LLC.
SONS AND DAUGHTERS OF THE MOST HIGH PUBLISHERS ®

Oh, Gracious Most High Heavenly father, Holy is your name, Your Will Be Done Now and Forever!

Therefore, as a person (**In-Div-Dual (I)** (**Am** means: <u>you exist</u> <u>as an "I" in the first-person address to oneself, as Me or Myself</u>) as a child of the Most High has an opportunity as a youth or adult to develop the habit of speaking the **True Vine (Yashu'a, Jesus), Life in the Power of the Tongue that Speaks Life INTO EXISTENCE by the "Will" of the Most High Heavenly Father <u>for your life</u>**! This is taught to adults by the Children of the Most High: Pristine Youth and Family Solutions, LLC as: "**True Vine (Yashu'a, Jesus) A**dults **L**earning **L**asting - **I**nspired **S**ustained, **I**nsightful; **A**greeable **M**indfulness (**All Is I Am**)." This is taught to youth by the Children of the Most High: Pristine Youth and Family Solutions, LLC as: "**True Vine (Yashu'a, Jesus) Youth: M**aking **I**ntentional **N**oble **D**ecisions (**M.I.N.D**)."

158

"And whatsoever we ask, we receive of him, because we keep his commandments, and do those things that are pleasing in his sight, KJV 1 John 3:22."

Beware of the Pink Assassin (Your Tongue): The True Vine
(Yashu'a, Jesus) Power of Life and Death is in the Tongue;
Speaking God's (אלהים Elŏhîym) "Will"
for Your Life into Existence!

CHILDREN OF THE MOST HIGH:
PRISTINE YOUTH AND FAMILY SOLUTIONS, LLC.
SONS AND DAUGHTERS OF THE MOST HIGH PUBLISHERS ®

*Oh, Gracious Most High Heavenly father, Holy is your name,
Your Will Be Done Now and Forever!*

The KJV bible book of 1st Corinthians chapter 2 verse 16; it states: "For who hath known **the mind** of the Lord, that he may instruct him? But we have **the mind** of Christ." If a person as an **in-di-vi-dual (in-the-visual)**, has **the mind of Christ**, is it **mine**? Or **my mind** too? What does the words **mine** and **mind** mean? According to Online American Heritage Dictionary (2020), **mine** is defined as: **"Used to indicate the one or ones belonging to me." Mind** is defined as: **"Individual consciousness, memory, or recollection." Mine** refers to the "**I**" principle that grows the "**I want to be seen or in-the-vis-u-al (in-di-vid-u-al). Mine** is also in reference to "**Individuality." Universal Love** is against **I**ndividuality, which is why the word "**Universe**" consists of the two syllables of "**Uni**" (**One**) **Verse** (**Against**) or "**ALL**" or "**The ALL**" is against "**I**ndividuality, Hughes 2020)."

159

"And whatsoever we ask, we receive of him, because we keep his commandments, and do those things that are pleasing in his sight, KJV 1 John 3:22."

Beware of the Pink Assassin (Your Tongue): The True Vine (Yashu'a, Jesus) Power of Life and Death is in the Tongue; Speaking God's (אלהים Elóhîym) "Will" for Your Life into Existence!

CHILDREN OF THE MOST HIGH:
PRISTINE YOUTH AND FAMILY SOLUTIONS, LLC.
SONS AND DAUGHTERS OF THE MOST HIGH PUBLISHERS ®

Oh, Gracious Most High Heavenly father, Holy is your name, Your Will Be Done Now and Forever!

"**Pride**", and the **Me, Myself** and **I Trinity** are the children of the "**EGO**, the KJV bible Greek Strong's Concordance#**1473** word: ἐγώ **egō** which means: **I, me, my**; a primary pronoun of the first person **I**" and are the greatest barriers to experiencing the Most High Heavenly Father through obedience to the "**Will**" and "**Commandments**" of the Most High . So, what did the Messiah Yashu'a (Jesus) mean when he said: "love the Most High Heavenly father with all of our mind and all of our heart?"

160

"And whatsoever we ask, we receive of him, because we keep his commandments, and do those things that are pleasing in his sight, KJV 1 John 3:22."

Beware of the Pink Assassin (Your Tongue): The True Vine (Yashu'a, Jesus) Power of Life and Death is in the Tongue; Speaking God's (אלהים Elóhîym) "Will" for Your Life into Existence!

CHILDREN OF THE MOST HIGH:
PRISTINE YOUTH AND FAMILY SOLUTIONS, LLC.
SONS AND DAUGHTERS OF THE MOST HIGH PUBLISHERS ®

Oh, Gracious Most High Heavenly father, Holy is your name, Your Will Be Done Now and Forever!

According to the KJV bible book of Matthew chapter 22 verse 36; it states: "Master, which is the great commandment in the law? the Messiah Yashu'a (Jesus) said: "Thou shalt love the Lord thy God with all thy <u>heart</u>, and with all thy soul, and with all thy <u>mind</u>, KJV Matthew 22:37." According to the **KJV bible Greek Strong's Concordance "#2588, καρδία Kardia** is the word for "**heart**". **Kardia** means: that organ in the animal body or human body which is the center of the circulation of the blood, and hence was regarded as the seat of physical life denotes the **center of all physical and spiritual life**. The KJV bible Greek Strong's Concordance #1271, διάνοια **Dianoia** is the word for "**mind**". **Dianoia** means: faculty of understanding, thinking and thoughts." According to the KJV bible book of Isaiah chapter 26 verse 3; it states with Aramic (Hebrew) excerpts:

26:3 יֵצֶר סָמוּךְ תִּצֹּר שָׁלוֹם שָׁלוֹם כִּי בְךָ בָּטוּחַ:

161

"And whatsoever we ask, we receive of him, because we keep his commandments, and do those things that are pleasing in his sight, KJV 1 John 3:22."

Beware of the Pink Assassin (Your Tongue): The True Vine (Yashu'a, Jesus) Power of Life and Death is in the Tongue; Speaking God's (אלהים Elohîym) "Will" for Your Life into Existence!

CHILDREN OF THE MOST HIGH:
PRISTINE YOUTH AND FAMILY SOLUTIONS, LLC.
SONS AND DAUGHTERS OF THE MOST HIGH PUBLISHERS ®

Oh, Gracious Most High Heavenly father, Holy is your name, Your Will Be Done Now and Forever!

"Thou wilt keep him in perfect peace, **whose mind** is stayed on thee: because he trusteth in thee." According to the **KJV bible Hebrew Strong's Concordance #3336**, is יֵצֶר **Yetser** for the phrase "**whose mind**." יֵצֶר **Yetser** means: form, framing, purpose, framework, thing framed, imagination, mind, work: framed purpose, imagination, device (intellectual framework)." According to the KJV bible book of 1st Corinthians chapter 2 verse 16; it states: "For who hath known **the mind** of the Lord, that he may instruct him? But we have **the mind** of Christ."

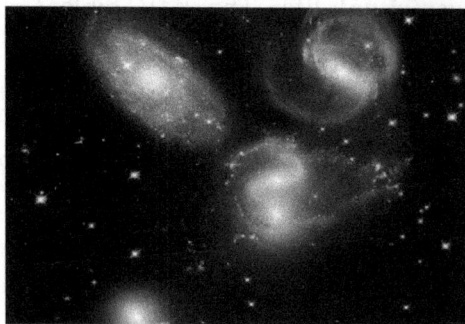

162

"And whatsoever we ask, we receive of him, because we keep his commandments, and do those things that are pleasing in his sight, KJV 1 John 3:22."

Beware of the Pink Assassin (Your Tongue): The True Vine
(Yashu'a, Jesus) Power of Life and Death is in the Tongue;
Speaking God's (אלהים Elóhîym) "Will"
for Your Life into Existence!

CHILDREN OF THE MOST HIGH:
PRISTINE YOUTH AND FAMILY SOLUTIONS, LLC.
SONS AND DAUGHTERS OF THE MOST HIGH PUBLISHERS ®

Oh, Gracious Most High Heavenly father, Holy is your name,
Your Will Be Done Now and Forever!

The **KJV bible Greek Strong's Concordance#3563**, is νοῦς

Nous for the phrase "**the mind**." νοῦς **Nous**, means: the mind,

comprising alike the faculties of perceiving and understanding

and those of feeling, judging, determining the intellectual

faculty, the understanding reason in the narrower sense, as the

capacity for spiritual truth, the higher powers of the soul, the

faculty of perceiving divine things, of recognizing goodness

and of hating evil the power of considering and judging soberly,

calmly and impartially a particular mode of thinking and

judging, thoughts, feelings, purposes, desires; the intellect,

mind (divine thought, or will)." A person speaks as a reflection

of how he or she thinks. So, the "**Christ Mind**" is reflected in

the words of the Messiah Yashu'a (Jesus) when he said: "Thou

shalt love the Lord thy God with all thy <u>heart</u>, and with all

thy soul, and with all thy <u>mind</u>."

163

"And whatsoever we ask, we receive of him,
because we keep his commandments, and do those
things that are pleasing in his sight, KJV 1 John 3:22."

Beware of the Pink Assassin (Your Tongue): The True Vine
(Yashu'a, Jesus) Power of Life and Death is in the Tongue;
Speaking God's (אלהים Elôhîym) "Will"
for Your Life into Existence!

CHILDREN OF THE MOST HIGH:
PRISTINE YOUTH AND FAMILY SOLUTIONS, LLC.
SONS AND DAUGHTERS OF THE MOST HIGH PUBLISHERS ®

Oh, Gracious Most High Heavenly father, Holy is your name,
Your Will Be Done Now and Forever!

**The mind and the heart have to be as one in active divine
love for the Most High Heavenly Father only**! This occurs
with each heartbeat, each breath, and when a person most
frequent, moment to moment intentional thinking, mental
focus, predominate thoughts, and heart divine love are only
focused on the Most High Heavenly Father, the Creator of All
of the boundless universes! Therefore, each child of the Most
High has an opportunity to get to **"Know Thyself"** and will
inevitably have to choose between, whether he or she values
"Mine" or the **"Christ Mind"** more if he or she seeks to <u>be
very successful at</u> **Mind Gardening in the Creative Garden
of Will (Your Mind) to grow the habit of speaking the True
Vine (Yashu'a, Jesus) Power of Life INTO EXISTENCE by
the "Will" of the Most High Heavenly Father <u>for your life</u>**!

164
**"And whatsoever we ask, we receive of him,
because we keep his commandments, and do those
things that are pleasing in his sight, KJV 1 John 3:22."**

Beware of the Pink Assassin (Your Tongue): The True Vine
(Yashu'a, Jesus) Power of Life and Death is in the Tongue;
Speaking God's (אלהים Elohîym) "Will"
for Your Life into Existence!

CHILDREN OF THE MOST HIGH:
PRISTINE YOUTH AND FAMILY SOLUTIONS, LLC.
SONS AND DAUGHTERS OF THE MOST HIGH PUBLISHERS ®

*Oh, Gracious Most High Heavenly father, Holy is your name,
Your Will Be Done Now and Forever!*

Chapter 8: If You Have Two Eyes (even if you can only see through one), Two Ears, and One Mouth; Look and Listen, Twice as Much as You Speak!

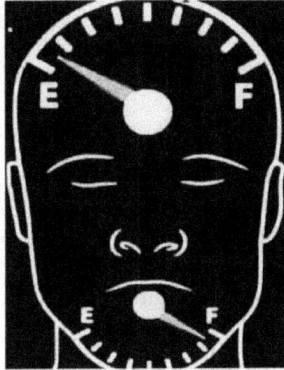

How can the children of the Most High avoid utilizing the Power of the Tongue to Speak Death into existence? We must learn to make and take the time every day to practice: Silence-being physically still, Reading-being spiritually still, Listening-being emotionally still, and Watching-being mentally still.

165

"And whatsoever we ask, we receive of him, because we keep his commandments, and do those things that are pleasing in his sight, KJV 1 John 3:22."

Beware of the Pink Assassin (Your Tongue): The True Vine
(Yashu'a, Jesus) Power of Life and Death is in the Tongue;
Speaking God's (אלהים Elohíym) "Will"
for Your Life into Existence!

CHILDREN OF THE MOST HIGH:
PRISTINE YOUTH AND FAMILY SOLUTIONS, LLC.
SONS AND DAUGHTERS OF THE MOST HIGH PUBLISHERS ®

*Oh, Gracious Most High Heavenly father, Holy is your name,
Your Will Be Done Now and Forever!*

These are the **schools of the wise children of the Most High** who are on an inner journey on a narrow path back to the Most High Heavenly Father through the Messiah Yashu'a (Jesus) who is the way, the truth, and the life and no person can get to the Most High Heavenly Father except through him. Consistent daily practice of these **schools of the wise children of the Most High disciplines**, leads to us balancing our lives, and empowers us to let go of all the **d**esires, **i**gnorance, **e**motions, **t**houghts, and **s**peaking (**d.i.e.t.s.**) that prevents us from the silence necessary to have a peace of mind that is essential to **growing the habit in your Creative Garden of Will (Your Mind), of the True Vine (Yashu'a, Jesus) Speaking Life into existence by the "Will" of the Most High for your life through the Power of your Tongue!**

166
**"And whatsoever we ask, we receive of him,
because we keep his commandments, and do those
things that are pleasing in his sight, KJV 1 John 3:22."**

Beware of the Pink Assassin (Your Tongue): The True Vine (Yashu'a, Jesus) Power of Life and Death is in the Tongue; Speaking God's (אלהים Elóhîym) "Will" for Your Life into Existence!

CHILDREN OF THE MOST HIGH:
PRISTINE YOUTH AND FAMILY SOLUTIONS, LLC.
SONS AND DAUGHTERS OF THE MOST HIGH PUBLISHERS ®

Oh, Gracious Most High Heavenly father, Holy is your name, Your Will Be Done Now and Forever!

The Messiah Yashu'a (Jesus) said: "I am the way, the truth, and the life: no man (the word for man is: Οὐδείς Oudeís, pronounced as: **Oo-dice'**; and **means: not even one (man, woman, child, or thing), none, nobody, nothing: not any at all**), cometh unto the Father, but by me, KJV John 14:6." In the KJV bible book of Matthew chapter 7 verses 13-14; it states: "Enter ye in at the strait gate: for wide is the gate, and broad is the way, that leadeth to destruction, and many there be which go in there at. Because strait is the gate, and narrow is the way, which leadeth unto life, and few there be that find it." The **True Vine (Yashu'a, Jesus) Life in the Power of the Tongue of Speaking Life words, have the power to heal!**

167

"And whatsoever we ask, we receive of him, because we keep his commandments, and do those things that are pleasing in his sight, KJV 1 John 3:22."

Beware of the Pink Assassin (Your Tongue): The True Vine (Yashu'a, Jesus) Power of Life and Death is in the Tongue; Speaking God's (אלהים Elôhîym) "Will" for Your Life into Existence!

CHILDREN OF THE MOST HIGH:
PRISTINE YOUTH AND FAMILY SOLUTIONS, LLC.
SONS AND DAUGHTERS OF THE MOST HIGH PUBLISHERS &

Oh, Gracious Most High Heavenly father, Holy is your name, Your Will Be Done Now and Forever!

For Example: In the KJV bible book of Matthew chapter 4 verse 4; the Messiah Yashu'a (Jesus) said: "It is written, **Man (ἄνθρωπος Anthrōpos - a human being)** shall not live by bread alone, but by every word that proceedeth out of the mouth of God." "When the even was come, they brought unto him many that were possessed with devils: **and he cast out the spirits with his word, and healed all that were sick**, KJV Matthew 8:16." "The centurion answered and said, Lord, I am not worthy that thou shouldest come under my roof: **but speak the word only, and my servant shall be healed**. KJV Matthew 8:8." In the KJV bible book of Revelation chapter 1 verses 14-15; it states: "His head and his hairs were white like wool, as white as snow; and his eyes were as a flame of fire; And his feet like unto fine brass, as if they burned in a furnace; **and his voice as the sound of many waters**."

168

"And whatsoever we ask, we receive of him, because we keep his commandments, and do those things that are pleasing in his sight, KJV 1 John 3:22."

Beware of the Pink Assassin (Your Tongue): The True Vine (Yashu'a, Jesus) Power of Life and Death is in the Tongue; Speaking God's (אלהים Elŏhîym) "Will" for Your Life into Existence!

CHILDREN OF THE MOST HIGH:
PRISTINE YOUTH AND FAMILY SOLUTIONS, LLC.
SONS AND DAUGHTERS OF THE MOST HIGH PUBLISHERS ®

Oh, Gracious Most High Heavenly father, Holy is your name, Your Will Be Done Now and Forever!

Keeping in mind, that one of "**the Word** (λóγος **Logos**)" definitions is: **Divine mind**" which Hughes (2020) expounded on as **Living Water Mentality – Mind, thought waves which can produce sound as Rhythm** in the book entitled: "**Mind Gardening in the Creative Garden of Will (Your Mind) to Grow a Living Water Mentality**" book.

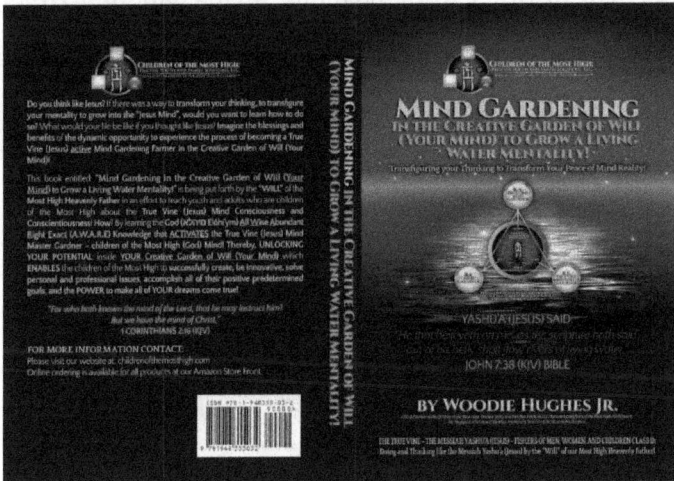

169

"And whatsoever we ask, we receive of him, because we keep his commandments, and do those things that are pleasing in his sight, KJV 1 John 3:22."

Beware of the Pink Assassin (Your Tongue): The True Vine (Yashu'a, Jesus) Power of Life and Death is in the Tongue; Speaking God's (אלהים Elŏhîym) "Will" for Your Life into Existence!

CHILDREN OF THE MOST HIGH:
PRISTINE YOUTH AND FAMILY SOLUTIONS, LLC.
SONS AND DAUGHTERS OF THE MOST HIGH PUBLISHERS ®

Oh, Gracious Most High Heavenly father, Holy is your name, Your Will Be Done Now and Forever!

The KJV bible Greek Strong's Concordance "#1100 is γλῶσσα Glōssa for the word: "tongue" (pronounced as: Gloce-sah'). γλῶσσα Glōssa is defined as: **the tongue, a member of the body, an organ of speech, a tongue - the language or dialect used by a particular people distinct from that of other nations.**" So, according to the Mayo Clinic (2020), "**Speech occurs** when air flows from the lungs, up the windpipe (trachea) and through the voice box (larynx). This causes the vocal cords to vibrate, <u>**creating sound**</u>. <u>**Sound**</u> is shaped into words by the muscles controlling the soft palate, tongue and lips."

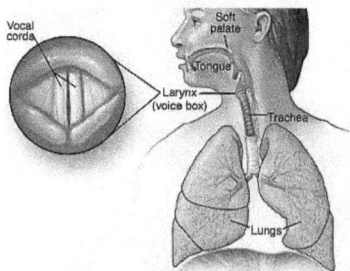

170

"And whatsoever we ask, we receive of him, because we keep his commandments, and do those things that are pleasing in his sight, KJV 1 John 3:22."

Beware of the Pink Assassin (Your Tongue): The True Vine (Yashu'a, Jesus) Power of Life and Death is in the Tongue; Speaking God's (אלהים Elóhîym) "Will" for Your Life into Existence!

CHILDREN OF THE MOST HIGH:
PRISTINE YOUTH AND FAMILY SOLUTIONS, LLC.
SONS AND DAUGHTERS OF THE MOST HIGH PUBLISHERS ®

Oh, Gracious Most High Heavenly father, Holy is your name, Your Will Be Done Now and Forever!

So, from the aforementioned verses, **words can heal**. **Verbal words are heard by way of sound**. Their **tone** sends **sound waves into the atmosphere** (Morse, 1948). Therefore, **verbal words can send positive or negative sound waves into the atmosphere, and words can inspire the mind and comfort the heart; or words can agitate the mind and cause discomfort to the heart** (Harris, 2010). For more information about how sound can heal, seek out the book entitled: "**Healing and Freedom THROUGH THESE SACRED TONE MASTERS**" written by: Jacqueline D. Harris!

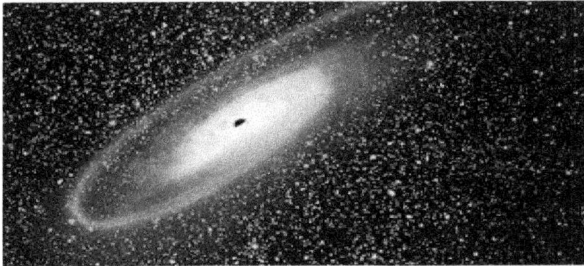

171

"And whatsoever we ask, we receive of him, because we keep his commandments, and do those things that are pleasing in his sight, KJV 1 John 3:22."

Beware of the Pink Assassin (Your Tongue): The True Vine (Yashu'a, Jesus) Power of Life and Death is in the Tongue;
Speaking God's (אלהים Elŏhîym) "Will" for Your Life into Existence!

Oh, Gracious Most High Heavenly father, Holy is your name, Your Will Be Done Now and Forever!

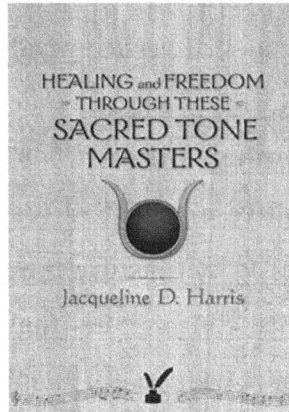

So, from the aforementioned, sound produces tones which when spoken by the Messiah Yashu'a (Jesus) as the sound of many waters, healed the sick and removed demons out of people. Our best sound is produced from diaphragm speaking which occurs from diaphragm breathing which increases oxygen in the blood, can lower blood pressure, and can assist with reducing stress (Yue, Gong, Zhang, Duan, Shi, & Li, (2017). "Diaphragmatic breathing (also called "abdominal breathing" or "belly breathing") encourages full oxygen exchange — that is, the beneficial trade of incoming oxygen for outgoing carbon dioxide."

172

"And whatsoever we ask, we receive of him, because we keep his commandments, and do those things that are pleasing in his sight, KJV 1 John 3:22."

Beware of the Pink Assassin (Your Tongue): The True Vine (Yashu'a, Jesus) Power of Life and Death is in the Tongue; Speaking God's (אלהים Elohîym) "Will" for Your Life into Existence!

CHILDREN OF THE MOST HIGH:
PRISTINE YOUTH AND FAMILY SOLUTIONS, LLC.
SONS AND DAUGHTERS OF THE MOST HIGH PUBLISHERS ®

Oh, Gracious Most High Heavenly father, Holy is your name, Your Will Be Done Now and Forever!

The "**Healing and Freedom THROUGH THESE SACRED TONE MASTERS**" book was a true blessing sent to help heal humanity. Many people want to be happy, loved and healthy. Many of us have been hurt before and so many of us have experienced challenges with our health. The "**Healing and Freedom THROUGH THESE SACRED TONE MASTERS**" book may help each reader to heal, overcome their fears and be successful in all of their endeavors. If a person reads this book with an open mind, an open and honest heart, the voices of the **Healing Tone Masters** may speak to your heart, which takes the reader on an inner journey to **know thyself**. Reading about Jackie's relationship with Ms. Octavia Butler brought tears to my eyes as I could feel her pain through her writings about Ms. Butler's (her friend and mentor) transition from this physical realm.

173

"And whatsoever we ask, we receive of him, because we keep his commandments, and do those things that are pleasing in his sight, KJV 1 John 3:22."

Beware of the Pink Assassin (Your Tongue): The True Vine (Yashu'a, Jesus) Power of Life and Death is in the Tongue; **Speaking God's (אלהים Elŏhîym) "Will" for Your Life into Existence!**

CHILDREN OF THE MOST HIGH:
PRISTINE YOUTH AND FAMILY SOLUTIONS, LLC.
SONS AND DAUGHTERS OF THE MOST HIGH PUBLISHERS ®

Oh, Gracious Most High Heavenly father, Holy is your name,
Your Will Be Done Now and Forever!

Ms. Butler instilled the virtue of patience in Jackie's heart. Like Jackie, I have also been striving to master exercising patience in all that The Most High allows me to do. After almost dying in February 2012, and receiving a diagnosis of Chrohn's Disease; Jackie's book helped me to overstand and practice the virtue of patience that she wrote about in her book. Practicing patience is a matter of life and death for me now to help me to avoid stress and any future Chrohn's flare ups. Patience is a virtue of success! In 2012, the "**Healing and Freedom THROUGH THESE SACRED TONE MASTERS**" book also helped me to face the first spirit of fear which is the spirit of Infirmity which causes some members of humanity to react to basic trials and tribulations of life by getting mentally, spiritually, emotionally or physically sick.

174
"And whatsoever we ask, we receive of him, because we keep his commandments, and do those things that are pleasing in his sight, KJV 1 John 3:22."

Beware of the Pink Assassin (Your Tongue): The True Vine
(Yashu'a, Jesus) Power of Life and Death is in the Tongue;
Speaking God's (אלהים Elóhîym) "Will"
for Your Life into Existence!

CHILDREN OF THE MOST HIGH:
PRISTINE YOUTH AND FAMILY SOLUTIONS, LLC.
SONS AND DAUGHTERS OF THE MOST HIGH PUBLISHERS ®

*Oh, Gracious Most High Heavenly father, Holy is your name,
Your Will Be Done Now and Forever!*

Ledisi Young reminded me that: **"Fearlessness requires total
trust in your Creator."** Change is the only absolute in the
Universe. **Dianne Reeves** helped me to see **how futile it was
for me to resist change** to the point of making myself
physically sick. **Lalah Hathaway** reminded me to: **"Live life
making the best of every moment/situation, as they can end
up fleeting or lasting a life time."** Dr. Maya Angelou
reminded me how important it is to: **"Be honest with who you
are first and how you feel about situations that occur in your
life." Anita Baker** taught me that **it takes great discipline and
mental focus to sometimes put your professional goals on
hold in order to fulfill your purpose as it relates beginning
a family. Maysa Leak** reminded me of **the importance of
having faith in your Creator**. "Maysa had to have faith in her
Creator to leave her only child in a hospital in another country."

175

**"And whatsoever we ask, we receive of him,
because we keep his commandments, and do those
things that are pleasing in his sight, KJV 1 John 3:22."**

Beware of the Pink Assassin (Your Tongue): The True Vine
(Yashu'a, Jesus) Power of Life and Death is in the Tongue;
Speaking God's (אלהים Elóhîym) "Will"
for Your Life into Existence!

CHILDREN OF THE MOST HIGH:
PRISTINE YOUTH AND FAMILY SOLUTIONS, LLC.
SONS AND DAUGHTERS OF THE MOST HIGH PUBLISHERS ®

*Oh, Gracious Most High Heavenly father, Holy is your name,
Your Will Be Done Now and Forever!*

Cassandra Wilson reminded me to: **"Trust in The Most High. No matter how things may appear and no matter what someone else may say**, I have to trust." Thank you, Jackie, for the many sacrifices that you made to share the Healing and Freedom Through these Sacred Tone Masters book with all members of humanity; this book is one of the best books that I ever read in my life! **So, if you have two eyes (even if you can only see through one), two ears, and one mouth; look and listen, twice as much as you speak!** This is an essential action that must occur repeatedly, each moment of your life in order **to grow the habit in your Creative Garden of Will (Your Mind) of the True Vine (Yashu'a, Jesus) Power in the Tongue of Speaking Life into existence by the "Will" of the Most High for your life!**

176
"And whatsoever we ask, we receive of him, because we keep his commandments, and do those things that are pleasing in his sight, KJV 1 John 3:22."

Beware of the Pink Assassin (Your Tongue): The True Vine
(Yashu'a, Jesus) Power of Life and Death is in the Tongue;
Speaking God's (אלהים Elôhîym) "Will"
for Your Life into Existence!

CHILDREN OF THE MOST HIGH:
PRISTINE YOUTH AND FAMILY SOLUTIONS, LLC.
SONS AND DAUGHTERS OF THE MOST HIGH PUBLISHERS ®

*Oh, Gracious Most High Heavenly father, Holy is your name,
Your Will Be Done Now and Forever!*

Chapter 9: Speaking God's (אלהים Elôhîym) "Will" for Your Life into Existence!

THE MESSIAH YASHU'A (JESUS)
SAID: "THINK NOT THAT I COME TO BRING
PEACE ON EARTH; I CAME NOT TO SEND
PEACE, BUT A SWORD!, KJV MATTHEW 10:34."

177

"And whatsoever we ask, we receive of him,
because we keep his commandments, and do those
things that are pleasing in his sight, KJV 1 John 3:22."

Beware of the Pink Assassin (Your Tongue): The True Vine (Yashu'a, Jesus) Power of Life and Death is in the Tongue; Speaking God's (אלהים Elôhîym) "Will" for Your Life into Existence!

CHILDREN OF THE MOST HIGH:
PRISTINE YOUTH AND FAMILY SOLUTIONS, LLC.
SONS AND DAUGHTERS OF THE MOST HIGH PUBLISHERS ®

Oh, Gracious Most High Heavenly father, Holy is your name, Your Will Be Done Now and Forever!

A Person Speaks as He or She Thinks in their Mind and Feels in their Heart! In this chapter, we will utilize the Online KJV bible Greek Strong's Concordance (2020), "**the Word (λόγος Logos**) definitions of: **The Divine Expression (Christ):—communication, as well of those things which are put together in thought, as of those which, having been thought gathered together in the mind, are expressed in words.**" Which are essential to **Speaking God's (אלהים Elôhîym) "Will" for Your Life into Existence!**

178

"And whatsoever we ask, we receive of him, because we keep his commandments, and do those things that are pleasing in his sight, KJV 1 John 3:22."

Beware of the Pink Assassin (Your Tongue): The True Vine
(Yashu'a, Jesus) Power of Life and Death is in the Tongue;
Speaking God's (אלהים Elŏhîym) "Will"
for Your Life into Existence!

CHILDREN OF THE MOST HIGH:
PRISTINE YOUTH AND FAMILY SOLUTIONS, LLC.
SONS AND DAUGHTERS OF THE MOST HIGH PUBLISHERS ®

Oh, Gracious Most High Heavenly father, Holy is your name,
Your Will Be Done Now and Forever!

What is Speaking in Tongues?

The **Messiah Yashu'a (Jesus)** <u>spoke</u> the **Aramic/Hebrew
language** and the **Galilaean/Syriac language** which are very
close in dialect. At the day of Pentecost, in the KJV bible book of
Acts chapter 2, **the devout men were all filled with the Holy
Ghost**, and began to speak with other **tongues γλῶσσα Glōssa
(languages)**, <u>as the Spirit gave them utterance being able to
understand one another in Yashu'a (Jesus) Galilaean
language that he spoke</u>, which is why to the onlookers of this
miraculous event asked: "are not all these which speak
<u>Galilaeans</u>?" **Yashu'a (Jesus) did not speak the English and
Greek languages**. Now that we know from the previous verse that
tongues γλῶσσα Glōssa, means "**languages**."

179

**"And whatsoever we ask, we receive of him,
because we keep his commandments, and do those
things that are pleasing in his sight, KJV 1 John 3:22."**

Beware of the Pink Assassin (Your Tongue): The True Vine
(Yashu'a, Jesus) Power of Life and Death is in the Tongue;
Speaking God's (אלהים Elõhîym) "Will"
for Your Life into Existence!

CHILDREN OF THE MOST HIGH:
PRISTINE YOUTH AND FAMILY SOLUTIONS, LLC.
SONS AND DAUGHTERS OF THE MOST HIGH PUBLISHERS ®

*Oh, Gracious Most High Heavenly father, Holy is your name,
Your Will Be Done Now and Forever!*

**As it relates to the Power of Life and Death Being in the
Tongue, Explain the Children of the Most High: Pristine
Youth and Family Solutions, LLC. 9 True Vine (Yashu'a,
Jesus) Spiritual Gifts?**

The 9 True Vine Yashu'a (Jesus) Spiritual Gifts are:

1. <u>**The Spirit of the Word of Wisdom**</u> (In the KJV bible
   book of 1st Corinthians chapter 12 verse 8).
2. <u>**The Spirit of the Word of Knowledge**</u> (In the KJV
   bible book of 1st Corinthians chapter 12 verse 8).
3. <u>**The Spirit of Faith**</u> (In the KJV bible book of 1st
   Corinthians chapter 12 verse 9).
4. <u>**The Spirit of Healing**</u> (In the KJV bible book of 1st
   Corinthians chapter 12 verse 9).
5. <u>**The Spirit of Working Miracles**</u> (In the KJV bible
   book of 1st Corinthians chapter 12 verse 10).
6. <u>**The Spirit of Prophecy**</u> (In the KJV bible book of 1st
   Corinthians chapter 12 verse 10).

**"And whatsoever we ask, we receive of him,
because we keep his commandments, and do those
things that are pleasing in his sight, KJV 1 John 3:22."**

Beware of the Pink Assassin (Your Tongue): The True Vine (Yashu'a, Jesus) Power of Life and Death is in the Tongue; Speaking God's (אלהים Elohîym) "Will" for Your Life into Existence!

CHILDREN OF THE MOST HIGH:
PRISTINE YOUTH AND FAMILY SOLUTIONS, LLC.
SONS AND DAUGHTERS OF THE MOST HIGH PUBLISHERS ®

Oh, Gracious Most High Heavenly father, Holy is your name, Your Will Be Done Now and Forever!

7. <u>**The Spirit of Discerning of Spirits**</u> (In the KJV bible book of 1st Corinthians chapter 12 verse 10).

8. <u>**The Spirit of Diverse kinds of Tongues**</u> (In the KJV bible book of 1st Corinthians chapter 12 verse 10).

9. <u>**The Spirit of Interpretation of Tongues**</u> (In the KJV bible book of 1st Corinthians chapter 12 verse 10).

181

"And whatsoever we ask, we receive of him, because we keep his commandments, and do those things that are pleasing in his sight, KJV 1 John 3:22."

Beware of the Pink Assassin (Your Tongue): The True Vine
(Yashu'a, Jesus) Power of Life and Death is in the Tongue;
Speaking God's (אלהים Elôhîym) "Will"
for Your Life into Existence!

*Oh, Gracious Most High Heavenly father, Holy is your name,
Your Will Be Done Now and Forever!*

So, since "**the Word** (λόγος **Logos**) definitions of: The Divine
Expression (Christ): —communication, as well of those things
which are put together in thought, as of those which, having
been thought gathered together in the mind, are expressed in
words, which are essential to Speaking God's (אלהים Elôhîym)
"Will" for Your Life into Existence; **The 9 True Vine Yashu'a
(Jesus) Spiritual (πνευματικός Pneumatikos) Gifts (χάρισμα
Charisma) are explained** as such: According to the Online
KJV Blue Letter bible Greek Strong's Concordance (2020),
"**#4152** is the word: "**Spiritual**" (πνευματικός **Pneumatikos**),
pronounced as**: Pnyoo-mat-ik-os'**, means: "**relating to the
human spirit, or rational soul, as part of the man which is
akin to God and serves as his instrument or organ that
which possesses the nature of the rational soul belonging to
a spirit.**"

182

**"And whatsoever we ask, we receive of him,
because we keep his commandments, and do those
things that are pleasing in his sight, KJV 1 John 3:22."**

Beware of the Pink Assassin (Your Tongue): The True Vine
(Yashu'a, Jesus) Power of Life and Death is in the Tongue;
Speaking God's (אלהים Elo'hîym) "Will"
for Your Life into Existence!

CHILDREN OF THE MOST HIGH:
PRISTINE YOUTH AND FAMILY SOLUTIONS, LLC.
SONS AND DAUGHTERS OF THE MOST HIGH PUBLISHERS ®

*Oh, Gracious Most High Heavenly father, Holy is your name,
Your Will Be Done Now and Forever!*

"**Or a being higher than man but inferior to God**, belonging to the Divine Spirit of God, the Holy Spirit, one who is filled with and governed by the Spirit of God, pertaining to the wind or breath; windy, exposed to the wind, blowing. "**#4586** is the word: "**Gifts**" (χάρισμα **Charisma**), pronounced as: (**Khä'-re-smä**), means: "a favor with which one receives without any merit of his own, the gift of divine grace, the gift of faith, knowledge, holiness, virtue, the economy of divine grace, by which the pardon of sin and eternal salvation is appointed to sinners in consideration of the merits of Christ laid hold of by faith, grace or gifts denoting extraordinary powers, the reception of which is due to the power of divine grace operating on their souls by the Holy Spirit."

183

**"And whatsoever we ask, we receive of him,
because we keep his commandments, and do those
things that are pleasing in his sight, KJV 1 John 3:22."**

Beware of the Pink Assassin (Your Tongue): The True Vine (Yashu'a, Jesus) Power of Life and Death is in the Tongue; **Speaking God's (אלהים Elòhîym) "Will" for Your Life into Existence!**

CHILDREN OF THE MOST HIGH:
PRISTINE YOUTH AND FAMILY SOLUTIONS, LLC.
SONS AND DAUGHTERS OF THE MOST HIGH PUBLISHERS ®

*Oh, Gracious Most High Heavenly father, Holy is your name,
Your Will Be Done Now and Forever!*

Therefore, the Online KJV Blue Letter bible Greek Strong's Concordance (2020), "**#4151** is the word: "**Spirit**" πνεῦμα **Pneûma**, pronounced as: **Pnyoo'-mah**, and means: the spirit, the vital principal by which the body is animated, the power by which the human being feels, thinks, decides; [the soul is the emotional you which differs from the spirit and the mind]. Devoid of all or at least all grosser matter, and possessed of the power of knowing, desiring, deciding, and acting, a life giving spirit, a spirit higher than a physical human being, but lower than God, an angel, used of demons, or evil spirits, who were conceived as inhabiting the bodies of human beings, the spiritual nature of Christ, the divine nature of Christ, a movement of air (a gentle blast) of the wind, hence the wind itself breath of nostrils or mouth."

184

"And whatsoever we ask, we receive of him, because we keep his commandments, and do those things that are pleasing in his sight, KJV 1 John 3:22."

Beware of the Pink Assassin (Your Tongue): The True Vine
(Yashu'a, Jesus) Power of Life and Death is in the Tongue;
Speaking God's (אלהים Elóhîym) "Will"
for Your Life into Existence!

CHILDREN OF THE MOST HIGH:
PRISTINE YOUTH AND FAMILY SOLUTIONS, LLC.
SONS AND DAUGHTERS OF THE MOST HIGH PUBLISHERS ®

*Oh, Gracious Most High Heavenly father, Holy is your name,
Your Will Be Done Now and Forever!*

The 9 True Vine Yashu'a (Jesus) Spiritual Gifts in the KJV bible book of 1st Corinthians chapter 12 verse 8-10 are: **The Spirit (πνεῦμα Pneûma) of the Word (λόγος Logos) of Wisdom (σοφία Sophia** – Wisdom (higher or lower, worldly or spiritual). **The Spirit (πνεῦμα Pneûma) of the Word (λόγος Logos) of Knowledge** (γνῶσις Gnōsis - knowing (the act), knowledge). **The Spirit (πνεῦμα Pneûma) of Faith (πίστις Pistis** - moral conviction, assurance, faith, fidelity). **The Spirit (πνεῦμα Pneûma) of Healing (ἴαμα Iama (Ee'-am-ah)** - a cure (the effect): —healing). **The Spirit (πνεῦμα Pneûma) of Working (ἐνέργημα Energēma (En-erg'-ay-mah)** - an effect: —operation, working), **Miracles (δύναμις Dynamis (Doo'-nam-is)** miraculous power (usually by implication, a miracle itself): —ability, abundance, meaning, might (-ily, -y, -y deed).

185

**"And whatsoever we ask, we receive of him,
because we keep his commandments, and do those
things that are pleasing in his sight, KJV 1 John 3:22."**

Beware of the Pink Assassin (Your Tongue): The True Vine (Yashu'a, Jesus) Power of Life and Death is in the Tongue; Speaking God's (אלהים Elohîym) "Will" for Your Life into Existence!

CHILDREN OF THE MOST HIGH:
PRISTINE YOUTH AND FAMILY SOLUTIONS, LLC.
SONS AND DAUGHTERS OF THE MOST HIGH PUBLISHERS ®

Oh, Gracious Most High Heavenly father, Holy is your name, Your Will Be Done Now and Forever!

The Spirit (πνεῦμα Pneûma) of Prophecy (προφητεία **Prophēteia (Prof-ay-ti'-ah)** - "prophecy"; prediction (scriptural or other): —prophecy, prophesying). **The Spirit (πνεῦμα Pneûma) of Discerning** (διάκρισις **Diakrisis (Dee-ak'-ree-sis)** a distinguishing, discerning, judging-not for the purpose of passing judgment on opinions, as to which one is to be preferred as the more correct, judicial estimation: —discern (-ing), disputation) **of Spirits (πνεῦμα Pneûma). The Spirit (πνεῦμα Pneûma) of Diverse kinds** (γένος **Genos – kin, diversity) of Tongues** (γλῶσσα **Glōssa (Gloce-sah')** - a tongue, language or languages). in the KJV bible book of 1st Corinthians chapter 12 verse 10). **The Spirit (πνεῦμα Pneûma) of Interpretation** (ἑρμηνεία **Hermēneia (Her-may-ni'-ah)** - translation: interpretation **of Tongues** (γλῶσσα **Glōssa** – languages) in the KJV bible book of 1st Corinthians chapter 12 verse 10)."

186

"And whatsoever we ask, we receive of him, because we keep his commandments, and do those things that are pleasing in his sight, KJV 1 John 3:22."

Beware of the Pink Assassin (Your Tongue): The True Vine
(Yashu'a, Jesus) Power of Life and Death is in the Tongue;
Speaking God's (אלהים Elôhîym) "Will"
for Your Life into Existence!

CHILDREN OF THE MOST HIGH:
PRISTINE YOUTH AND FAMILY SOLUTIONS, LLC.
SONS AND DAUGHTERS OF THE MOST HIGH PUBLISHERS ®

*Oh, Gracious Most High Heavenly father, Holy is your name,
Your Will Be Done Now and Forever!*

The **9 True Vine (Yashu'a, Jesus) Spiritual Gifts** enable the
children of the Most High **to best speak the Doctrine of the
Most High to the hearts and minds of people through what
they value the most**! So, the **9 True Vine (Yashu'a, Jesus)
Spiritual Gifts** will only help the children of the Most High
who have received any of the spiritual gifts; if they only live
and exist to be obedient to the commandments of the Most
High, focus whole-heartily through their divine love for the
Most High to do the Most High Heavenly Father's "**Will**" and
upkeep all of their personal and professional responsibilities
that align with the "**Will**" of the Most High! This is essential as
it relates to **Speaking God's (אלהים Elôhîym) "Will" for Your
Life into Existence!** So, as it relates to human life on the
physical realm (on earth), **what is more important than your
next breath, and your next heartbeat**? Therefore; **a person
can't speak like or be like, the Messiah Yashu'a (Christ,
Jesus) while they are still thinking, feeling and speaking like
the devil!**

187

**"And whatsoever we ask, we receive of him,
because we keep his commandments, and do those
things that are pleasing in his sight, KJV 1 John 3:22."**

Beware of the Pink Assassin (Your Tongue): The True Vine
(Yashu'a, Jesus) Power of Life and Death is in the Tongue;
Speaking God's (אלהים Elóhîym) "Will"
for Your Life into Existence!

CHILDREN OF THE MOST HIGH:
PRISTINE YOUTH AND FAMILY SOLUTIONS, LLC.
SONS AND DAUGHTERS OF THE MOST HIGH PUBLISHERS ®

Oh, Gracious Most High Heavenly father, Holy is your name,
Your Will Be Done Now and Forever!

In conclusion, the **Love Words** that are rooted in the
Foundation of the True Vine (Yashu'a, Jesus) Fruits of the
Spirit of Positive Character-Building Essentials are: <u>love</u>, <u>joy</u>,
<u>peace</u>, <u>longsuffering</u>, <u>gentleness</u>, <u>goodness</u>, <u>faith</u>, <u>Meekness</u>,
<u>temperance</u>. According Newberg and Walman (2012), "A
single word has the power to influence the expression of genes
that regulate the physical and emotional stress." So, according
to Dr. Newberg, words can change your brain (Newberg and
Walman, 2012). **Consequently,** our **thoughts**, **words**, **and**
actions will tremendously continue to influence the quality of
our life experiences!

188

"And whatsoever we ask, we receive of him,
because we keep his commandments, and do those
things that are pleasing in his sight, KJV 1 John 3:22."

Beware of the Pink Assassin (Your Tongue): The True Vine (Yashu'a, Jesus) Power of Life and Death is in the Tongue; Speaking God's (אלהים Elohîym) "Will" for Your Life into Existence!

CHILDREN OF THE MOST HIGH:
PRISTINE YOUTH AND FAMILY SOLUTIONS, LLC.
SONS AND DAUGHTERS OF THE MOST HIGH PUBLISHERS ®

Oh, Gracious Most High Heavenly father, Holy is your name, Your Will Be Done Now and Forever!

Therefore; it is **essential** for the children of the Most to incorporate these **love words, their meanings**, and **their synonyms into our minds, hearts**, and **into our everyday communications. The children of the Most High must continuously put the following words in A.C.T.I.O.N. (Activated, Conscious, Timely, Intentions, Obligated, Now) through all of our works, and in all that we are graciously blessed with the opportunity to do**: "On my own accord, I can of mine own self do nothing, I seek not mine own will, but the will of the Father which hath sent me" according to the Most High Heavenly Father's pre**ordained purpose** for your life." So, it is **essential** that the children of the Most High: **Beware** (Be Aware) **of the Pink Assassin** (Your Tongue); **by thinking, saying, and doing the aforementioned**, the True Vine (Yashu'a, Jesus) Power of Life and Death is SPOKEN INTO EXISTENCE by the "Will" of the Most High Heavenly Father for your life! **"And whatsoever we ask, we receive of him, because we keep his commandments, and do those things that are pleasing in his sight, KJV 1 John 3:22."**

189

"And whatsoever we ask, we receive of him, because we keep his commandments, and do those things that are pleasing in his sight, KJV 1 John 3:22."

Beware of the Pink Assassin (Your Tongue): The True Vine (Yashu'a, Jesus) Power of Life and Death is in the Tongue; Speaking God's (אלהים Elohîym) "Will" for Your Life into Existence!

CHILDREN OF THE MOST HIGH:
PRISTINE YOUTH AND FAMILY SOLUTIONS, LLC.
SONS AND DAUGHTERS OF THE MOST HIGH PUBLISHERS ®

Oh, Gracious Most High Heavenly father, Holy is your name,
Your Will Be Done Now and Forever!

Appendix:
What is the Children of the Most High: Pristine Youth and Family Solutions, LLC. Proclamation?

"We greet all in peace with a sincere heart. We are non-violent and agree with the Reverend Dr. Martin Luther King Jr. when he said: "At the center of non-violence stands the principle of love." We stay sober, we don't drink alcohol, we don't become intoxicated, we eat healthy, we exercise, and we don't smoke anything for the body is a temple where the spirit of the Most High dwells; so, our bodies and minds must be in a state of cleanliness! We respect nature, we respect the laws of nature, and the Most High Heavenly Father who is the source of it all. We don't hate any race, creed, religion, or sexual orientation. We advocate that humanity practice being just to the depressed, in mind or circumstances, the poor, and underserved underrepresented members of humanity. We advocate that humanity practice defending the poor, motherless and fatherless from all injustices. We seek to help deliver the poor and needy out of the hands of the wicked by teaching them how to activate the latent potential in them through their inborn gifts, by learning and applying the Most High's doctrine in all that they do, through repentance, and through the acceptance of the Messiah Yashu'a (Jesus), and through the eternal obedience to the Most High Heavenly Father's "Will" and commandments. We seek to help empower members of humanity to take that which is evil and to turn it into good. We seek to work with all members of humanity to help make the world a safer, peaceful, healthy, and poverty free environment for all youth and all adults to live in; and we obey Yashu'a (Jesus) commandment to love one another."

190

"And whatsoever we ask, we receive of him, because we keep his commandments, and do those things that are pleasing in his sight, KJV 1 John 3:22."

Beware of the Pink Assassin (Your Tongue): The True Vine (Yashu'a, Jesus) Power of Life and Death is in the Tongue; Speaking God's (אלהים Elơhîym) "Will" for Your Life into Existence!

CHILDREN OF THE MOST HIGH:
PRISTINE YOUTH AND FAMILY SOLUTIONS, LLC.
SONS AND DAUGHTERS OF THE MOST HIGH PUBLISHERS ®

Oh, Gracious Most High Heavenly father, Holy is your name, Your Will Be Done Now and Forever!

Below is a Prayer of Repentance:

In the KJV bible book of Psalms chapter 51 verses 1-19; it states: "51 Have mercy upon me, O God, according to thy lovingkindness: according unto the multitude of thy tender mercies blot out my transgressions. [2] Wash me throughly from mine iniquity, and cleanse me from my sin. [3] For I acknowledge my transgressions: and my sin is ever before me. [4] Against thee, thee only, have I sinned, and done this evil in thy sight: that thou mightest be justified when thou speakest, and be clear when thou judgest. [5] Behold, I was shapen in iniquity; and in sin did my mother conceive me. [6] Behold, thou desirest truth in the inward parts: and in the hidden part thou shalt make me to know wisdom. [7] Purge me with hyssop, and I shall be clean: wash me, and I shall be whiter than snow."

"And whatsoever we ask, we receive of him, because we keep his commandments, and do those things that are pleasing in his sight, KJV 1 John 3:22."

Beware of the Pink Assassin (Your Tongue): The True Vine
(Yashu'a, Jesus) Power of Life and Death is in the Tongue;
Speaking God's (אלהים Elôhîym) "Will"
for Your Life into Existence!

CHILDREN OF THE MOST HIGH:
PRISTINE YOUTH AND FAMILY SOLUTIONS, LLC.
SONS AND DAUGHTERS OF THE MOST HIGH PUBLISHERS ®

*Oh, Gracious Most High Heavenly father, Holy is your name,
Your Will Be Done Now and Forever!*

[8] Make me to hear joy and gladness; that the bones which thou hast broken may rejoice. [9] Hide thy face from my sins, and blot out all mine iniquities. [10] Create in me a clean heart, O God; and renew a right spirit within me. [11] Cast me not away from thy presence; and take not thy holy spirit from me. [12] Restore unto me the joy of thy salvation; and uphold me with thy free spirit. [13] Then will I teach transgressors thy ways; and sinners shall be converted unto thee. [14] Deliver me from bloodguiltiness, O God, thou God of my salvation: and my tongue shall sing aloud of thy righteousness. [15] O Lord, open thou my lips; and my mouth shall shew forth thy praise. [16] For thou desirest not sacrifice; else would I give it: thou delightest not in burnt offering. [17] The sacrifices of God are a broken spirit: a broken and a contrite heart, O God, thou wilt not despise."

192

**"And whatsoever we ask, we receive of him,
because we keep his commandments, and do those
things that are pleasing in his sight, KJV 1 John 3:22."**

Beware of the Pink Assassin (Your Tongue): The True Vine (Yashu'a, Jesus) Power of Life and Death is in the Tongue; Speaking God's (אלהים Elóhîym) "Will" for Your Life into Existence!

CHILDREN OF THE MOST HIGH:
PRISTINE YOUTH AND FAMILY SOLUTIONS, LLC.
SONS AND DAUGHTERS OF THE MOST HIGH PUBLISHERS ®

Oh, Gracious Most High Heavenly father, Holy is your name, Your Will Be Done Now and Forever!

"¹⁸ Do good in thy good pleasure unto Zion: build thou the walls of Jerusalem. ¹⁹ Then shalt thou be pleased with the sacrifices of righteousness, with burnt offering and whole burnt offering: then shall they offer bullocks upon thine altar."

193

"And whatsoever we ask, we receive of him, because we keep his commandments, and do those things that are pleasing in his sight, KJV 1 John 3:22."

Beware of the Pink Assassin (Your Tongue): The True Vine (Yashu'a, Jesus) Power of Life and Death is in the Tongue; Speaking God's (אלהים Elóhîym) "Will" for Your Life into Existence!

CHILDREN OF THE MOST HIGH:
PRISTINE YOUTH AND FAMILY SOLUTIONS, LLC.
SONS AND DAUGHTERS OF THE MOST HIGH PUBLISHERS ®

Oh, Gracious Most High Heavenly father, Holy is your name,
Your Will Be Done Now and Forever!

In the KJV bible book of John chapter 14 verse 6; the Messiah Yashu'a (Jesus) said: "I am the way the truth, and the life: no man cometh unto the Father, but by me." However, according to the KJV bible book of John chapter 6 verse 44; only the Most High Heavenly Father can lead a person to the Messiah Yashu'a (Jesus). The Messiah Yashu'a (Jesus) said: "No man [person] can come to me, except the Father which hath sent me draw him: and I will raise him up at the last day." In the KJV bible book of John chapter 14 verse 21; the Messiah Yashu'a (Jesus) said: "He [or she] that hath my commandments, and keepeth them, he [or she] it is that loveth me: and he [or she] that loveth me shall be loved of my Father, and I will love him [or her], and will manifest myself to him [or her]."

194

"And whatsoever we ask, we receive of him,
because we keep his commandments, and do those
things that are pleasing in his sight, KJV 1 John 3:22."

Beware of the Pink Assassin (Your Tongue): The True Vine
(Yashu'a, Jesus) Power of Life and Death is in the Tongue;
Speaking God's (אלהים Elŏhîym) "Will"
for Your Life into Existence!

CHILDREN OF THE MOST HIGH:
PRISTINE YOUTH AND FAMILY SOLUTIONS, LLC.
SONS AND DAUGHTERS OF THE MOST HIGH PUBLISHERS ®

Oh, Gracious Most High Heavenly father, Holy is your name,
Your Will Be Done Now and Forever!

All obedient children of the Most High are seeking the
Kingdom of God and the Messiah Yashu'a (the True Vine,
Jesus), who will take those who have repented, accepted him as
their personal savior, and received the holy spirit, to the Most
High Heavenly Father. Once a person has accepted the Messiah
Yashu'a (Jesus) as their personal savior, there is a Kingdom of
God inside of them, but not there exclusively; and they are
always being attacked by the children of the devil. "Love gives
naught but itself and takes naught but from itself. Love
possesses not nor would it be possessed; For love is sufficient
unto love." (Gibran, 1968).

195

"And whatsoever we ask, we receive of him,
because we keep his commandments, and do those
things that are pleasing in his sight, KJV 1 John 3:22."

Beware of the Pink Assassin (Your Tongue): The True Vine
(Yashu'a, Jesus) Power of Life and Death is in the Tongue;
Speaking God's (אלהים Elohíym) "Will"
for Your Life into Existence!

CHILDREN OF THE MOST HIGH:
PRISTINE YOUTH AND FAMILY SOLUTIONS, LLC.
SONS AND DAUGHTERS OF THE MOST HIGH PUBLISHERS ®

Oh, Gracious Most High Heavenly father, Holy is your name,
Your Will Be Done Now and Forever!

What are the True Vine (Yashu'a, Jesus) Mind Gardening
Daily Individual or Family Household Habits of Success?
The True Vine (Yashu'a, Jesus) Mind Gardening Daily
Individual or Family Household Habits of Success are:

1. Obey the Most High Heavenly Father's will and
   commandments now and forever!

2. Love the Most High Heavenly Father with all of your
   heart, all of your spirit, all of your soul, all of your mind,
   and all of your entire being!

3. Decrease so that the Spirit of the Messiah Yashu'a
   (Jesus) can increase in you!

4. Do unto others as you would want others to do unto you!

5. Always think positive!

6. Always be positive!

7. Always have a positive attitude!

196

"And whatsoever we ask, we receive of him,
because we keep his commandments, and do those
things that are pleasing in his sight, KJV 1 John 3:22."

Beware of the Pink Assassin (Your Tongue): The True Vine
(Yashu'a, Jesus) Power of Life and Death is in the Tongue;
Speaking God's (אלהים Elóhîym) "Will"
for Your Life into Existence!

CHILDREN OF THE MOST HIGH:
PRISTINE YOUTH AND FAMILY SOLUTIONS, LLC.
SONS AND DAUGHTERS OF THE MOST HIGH PUBLISHERS ®

*Oh, Gracious Most High Heavenly father, Holy is your name,
Your Will Be Done Now and Forever!*

8. Open your heart before you open your mouth!

9. Remember, words should be soft, not hard!

10. It's nice to be important, but it is more important to be nice!

11. Mine your mind for the jewels of your soul!

12. Pray together daily!

13. Eat together in the same room a minimum of once a week!

14. Observe the Sabbath (Shu-Bat) weekly as a family!

15. Study and read the scriptures of the Most High as a family a minimum of once a week!

16. Watch a TV show or movie at home a minimum of once a week!

197

**"And whatsoever we ask, we receive of him,
because we keep his commandments, and do those
things that are pleasing in his sight, KJV 1 John 3:22."**

Beware of the Pink Assassin (Your Tongue): The True Vine
(Yashu'a, Jesus) Power of Life and Death is in the Tongue;
Speaking God's (אלהים Elŏhîym) "Will"
for Your Life into Existence!

CHILDREN OF THE MOST HIGH:
PRISTINE YOUTH AND FAMILY SOLUTIONS, LLC.
SONS AND DAUGHTERS OF THE MOST HIGH PUBLISHERS ®

Oh, Gracious Most High Heavenly father, Holy is your name,
Your Will Be Done Now and Forever!

17. Workout together as a family or ensure that all family members are working out on a weekly basis if their medical physicians have approved of them doing so.

18. Have family meetings once a week to discuss everyone's overall well-being, current events or anything else that is on any family member's mind, without the TV or any other electronic devices being on as a potential conversation distraction. One person speaks at a time, no arguing, no vulgarity, and all family members must respect each other!

19. Do some agreed upon, healthy, fun, and safe family event a minimum of once a month or weekly or bi-weekly together as a family.

198

"And whatsoever we ask, we receive of him,
because we keep his commandments, and do those
things that are pleasing in his sight, KJV 1 John 3:22."

Beware of the Pink Assassin (Your Tongue): The True Vine
(Yashu'a, Jesus) Power of Life and Death is in the Tongue;
Speaking God's (אלהים Elohîym) "Will"
for Your Life into Existence!

Oh, Gracious Most High Heavenly father, Holy is your name,
Your Will Be Done Now and Forever!

In the KJV bible book of Genesis, chapter 14 verse 18; it states: "And Melchizedek (Malkiy-Tsedeq, מַלְכִּי־צֶדֶק) king of Salem brought forth bread and wine: and he was the priest of the Most High (ELYOWN עֶלְיוֹן EL אֵל) God." In the KJV bible book of Psalms chapter 82 verse 6; states: "I have said, Ye are gods; and all of you are children **of the Most High** (is the KJV bible Hebrew Strong's Concordance#5945 which is the title: ELYOWN עֶלְיוֹן (the God) EL אֵל)." In the KJV bible book of Numbers chapter 23 verse 19; states: "**God (EL אֵל) is not a man**, that he should lie; neither the **son of man, that he should repent**: hath he said, and shall he not do it? or hath he spoken, and shall he not make it good?" However, **for clarification it is critical that all children of the Most High know that in the KJV bible book of Genesis Chapter 1 verse 1;** the original Aramic (Hebrew) word for "God" is "Elohiym" not the Most High (ELYOWN עֶלְיוֹן EL אֵל), the Sustainer, the Nourisher, the Provider of all Life, and the Omnipotent and the Omnipresent Creator of the boundless universes. So, the children of the Most High: Pristine Youth and Family Solutions, LLC. hopes that all children of the Most High acquire an overstanding of the differences between "God" ("אלהים 'Elohiym") in the KJV bible book of Genesis chapter 1 verse 1, "the LORD, יהוה Yěhovah, (Yahuwa, Yahweh, Jehovah, Yahayyu)" who repented to the Most High (ELYOWN עֶלְיוֹן EL אֵל) in the KJV bible book of Genesis chapter 6 verse 6; who is referred to as: "the LORD; and the יהוה Yěhovah "God" "אלהים 'Elohiym" who gets jealous in the KJV bible book of Exodus chapter 20 verse 5; ARE NOT TO BE CONFUSED AS BEING the Most High (ELYOWN עֶלְיוֹן EL אֵל), the Sustainer, the Nourisher, the Provider of all Life, and the Omnipotent and the Omnipresent Creator of the boundless universes who they all worship and do the 'Will" of!

199

"And whatsoever we ask, we receive of him,
because we keep his commandments, and do those
things that are pleasing in his sight, KJV 1 John 3:22."

Beware of the Pink Assassin (Your Tongue): The True Vine
(Yashu'a, Jesus) Power of Life and Death is in the Tongue;
Speaking God's (אלהים Elôhîym) "Will"
for Your Life into Existence!

CHILDREN OF THE MOST HIGH:
PRISTINE YOUTH AND FAMILY SOLUTIONS, LLC.
SONS AND DAUGHTERS OF THE MOST HIGH PUBLISHERS ®

Oh, Gracious Most High Heavenly father, Holy is your name,
Your Will Be Done Now and Forever!

Nothing would exist if you Oh Gracious Most High
Heavenly Father, The Creator didn't create it. You are
alone in Your Greatness; you have no partners that share
in your grace. To you all sovereignty is due and you are all
powerful over everything. We seek refuge in you, the ever
watchful Most High who hears and knows all things! Glory
be to you as many times as the number of things you have
created! All gratitude is due to you oh gracious Most High
Heavenly Father, you are the Creator and Sustainer of all
the boundless universes. You are the Yielder, and the most
Merciful. The Ruler of the Day of Decision.

200
**"And whatsoever we ask, we receive of him,
because we keep his commandments, and do those
things that are pleasing in his sight, KJV 1 John 3:22."**

Beware of the Pink Assassin (Your Tongue): The True Vine (Yashu'a, Jesus) Power of Life and Death is in the Tongue; Speaking God's (אלהים Elo̅hi̅ym) "Will" for Your Life into Existence!

CHILDREN OF THE MOST HIGH:
PRISTINE YOUTH AND FAMILY SOLUTIONS, LLC.
SONS AND DAUGHTERS OF THE MOST HIGH PUBLISHERS ®

Oh, Gracious Most High Heavenly father, Holy is your name,
Your Will Be Done Now and Forever!

It's you whom we worship and it is you alone whom we beseech for help, oh Guide, guide us to the narrow path (which reflects moral integrity and positive character traits in action) of the ones who stand straight, the narrow path of those who earned your grace not inclusive of those who brought an everlasting curse on themselves, those who conceal the facts of that which they know to be true in order to lead the sincere-hearted seekers of your truth astray. Amen

201

"And whatsoever we ask, we receive of him, because we keep his commandments, and do those things that are pleasing in his sight, KJV 1 John 3:22."

Beware of the Pink Assassin (Your Tongue): The True Vine
(Yashu'a, Jesus) Power of Life and Death is in the Tongue;
Speaking God's (אלהים Elohîym) "Will"
for Your Life into Existence!

*Oh, Gracious Most High Heavenly father, Holy is your name,
Your Will Be Done Now and Forever!*

About the Author

CHILDREN OF THE MOST HIGH:
PRISTINE YOUTH AND FAMILY SOLUTIONS, LLC.
SONS AND DAUGHTERS OF THE MOST HIGH PUBLISHERS ®

WOODIE
HUGHES JR.

CEO & FOUNDER
M.S. & B.S. IN CRIMINAL JUSTICE, ED.D. CANDIDATE

Mr. Hughes is a Servant of the Most High, Teacher of the
Most High's Doctrine, and a Youth and Adults Workshop
and Presentation Consultant.

📞 478-538-1918
✉ INFO@CHILDRENOFTHEMOSTHIGH.COM
🌐 CHILDRENOFTHEMOSTHIGH.COM
🐦 @WOODIEHUGHESJR9
f CHILDRENOFTHEMOSTHIGHPRISTINEYOUTHANDFAMSOLUTIONS

**"And whatsoever we ask, we receive of him,
because we keep his commandments, and do those
things that are pleasing in his sight, KJV 1 John 3:22."**

Beware of the Pink Assassin (Your Tongue): The True Vine (Yashu'a, Jesus) Power of Life and Death is in the Tongue;
Speaking God's (אלהים Elohîym) "Will" for Your Life into Existence!

CHILDREN OF THE MOST HIGH:
PRISTINE YOUTH AND FAMILY SOLUTIONS, LLC.
SONS AND DAUGHTERS OF THE MOST HIGH PUBLISHERS ®

Oh, Gracious Most High Heavenly father, Holy is your name, Your Will Be Done Now and Forever!

Mr. Woodie Hughes Jr. is the CEO & Founder of the Children of the Most High: Pristine Youth and Families Solutions LLC., Sons and Daughters of the Most High Publishers. Mr. Hughes is a Servant of the Most High and a Teacher of the Most High's Doctrine. Mr. Hughes is an Author who writes books that are being put forth by the will of the Most High Heavenly Father to inspire all youth and all adults **who are children of the Most High** to acquire the **competitive edge** against the children of devil. Mr. Hughes is a career university educator. Mr. Woodie Hughes Jr. and Mrs. Tonya Hughes have been happily married for 20 years and have a son and a daughter. Mr. Hughes is a veteran who has received a United States Army honorable discharge for his 8 years of service with the Illinois Army National Guard.

203

"And whatsoever we ask, we receive of him, because we keep his commandments, and do those things that are pleasing in his sight, KJV 1 John 3:22."

Beware of the Pink Assassin (Your Tongue): The True Vine (Yashu'a, Jesus) Power of Life and Death is in the Tongue; Speaking God's (אלהים Elóhîym) "Will" for Your Life into Existence!

CHILDREN OF THE MOST HIGH:
PRISTINE YOUTH AND FAMILY SOLUTIONS, LLC.
SONS AND DAUGHTERS OF THE MOST HIGH PUBLISHERS ®

Oh, Gracious Most High Heavenly father, Holy is your name, Your Will Be Done Now and Forever!

Mr. Hughes is the son of Mrs. Annette Hughes and Mr. Woodie Hughes Sr. who have been happily married for 50 years (as of 2020)! For over 27 years, Mr. Woodie Hughes Jr. has continued to be a devout student and teacher of the Most High's doctrine who is guided by the will of the Heavenly Father, and the Messiah Yashua's (Jesus) spirit of knowledge, spirit of wisdom, and spirit of true-faith all working as the same spirits (KJV bible book of 1st Corinthians chapter 12 verses 8-9) of the Messiah Yashu'a (Jesus) which has graciously been bestowed upon him. Mr. Hughes has accepted the Messiah Yashu'a (Jesus) as his savior and is in the Body of Christ!

204

"And whatsoever we ask, we receive of him, because we keep his commandments, and do those things that are pleasing in his sight, KJV 1 John 3:22."

Beware of the Pink Assassin (Your Tongue): The True Vine (Yashu'a, Jesus) Power of Life and Death is in the Tongue;
Speaking God's (אלהים Elóhíym) "Will"
for Your Life into Existence!

CHILDREN OF THE MOST HIGH:
PRISTINE YOUTH AND FAMILY SOLUTIONS, LLC.
SONS AND DAUGHTERS OF THE MOST HIGH PUBLISHERS ®

Oh, Gracious Most High Heavenly father, Holy is your name,
Your Will Be Done Now and Forever!

The Children of the Most High: Pristine Youth and Family Solutions, LLC. Books are available on Amazon and are listed below:

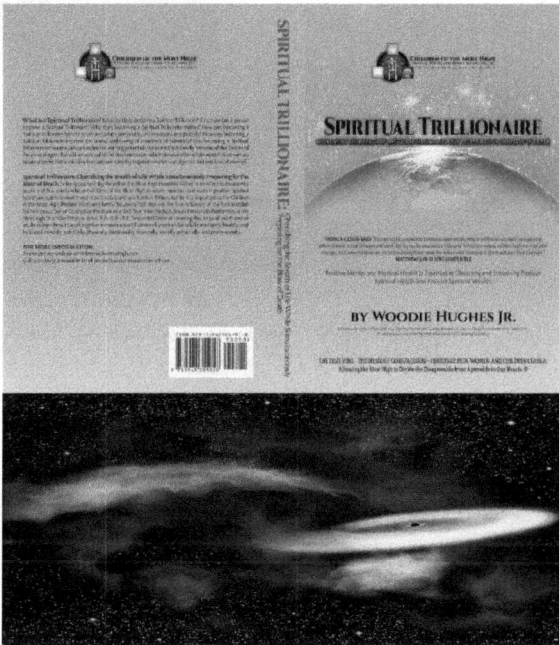

205

"And whatsoever we ask, we receive of him, because we keep his commandments, and do those things that are pleasing in his sight, KJV 1 John 3:22."

Beware of the Pink Assassin (Your Tongue): The True Vine (Yashu'a, Jesus) Power of Life and Death is in the Tongue; Speaking God's (אלהים Eloȟîym) "Will" for Your Life into Existence!

CHILDREN OF THE MOST HIGH:
PRISTINE YOUTH AND FAMILY SOLUTIONS, LLC.
SONS AND DAUGHTERS OF THE MOST HIGH PUBLISHERS ®

Oh, Gracious Most High Heavenly father, Holy is your name,
Your Will Be Done Now and Forever!

206

"And whatsoever we ask, we receive of him, because we keep his commandments, and do those things that are pleasing in his sight, KJV 1 John 3:22."

Beware of the Pink Assassin (Your Tongue): The True Vine (Yashu'a, Jesus) Power of Life and Death is in the Tongue; Speaking God's (אלהים Elohîym) "Will" for Your Life into Existence!

CHILDREN OF THE MOST HIGH:
PRISTINE YOUTH AND FAMILY SOLUTIONS, LLC.
SONS AND DAUGHTERS OF THE MOST HIGH PUBLISHERS ®

Oh, Gracious Most High Heavenly father, Holy is your name, Your Will Be Done Now and Forever!

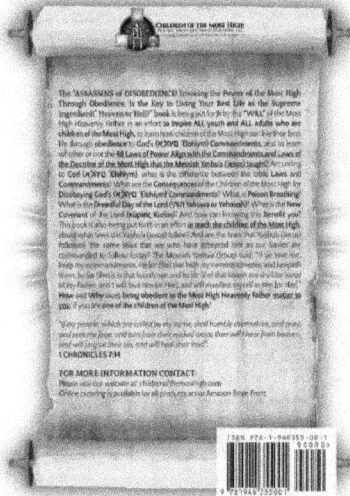

207

"And whatsoever we ask, we receive of him, because we keep his commandments, and do those things that are pleasing in his sight, KJV 1 John 3:22."

Beware of the Pink Assassin (Your Tongue): The True Vine
(Yashu'a, Jesus) Power of Life and Death is in the Tongue;
**Speaking God's (אלהים Elohîym) "Will"
for Your Life into Existence!**

CHILDREN OF THE MOST HIGH:
PRISTINE YOUTH AND FAMILY SOLUTIONS, LLC.
SONS AND DAUGHTERS OF THE MOST HIGH PUBLISHERS ®

*Oh, Gracious Most High Heavenly father, Holy is your name,
Your Will Be Done Now and Forever!*

208

**"And whatsoever we ask, we receive of him,
because we keep his commandments, and do those
things that are pleasing in his sight, KJV 1 John 3:22."**

Beware of the Pink Assassin (Your Tongue): The True Vine (Yashu'a, Jesus) Power of Life and Death is in the Tongue; **Speaking God's (אלהים Elôhîym) "Will" for Your Life into Existence!**

CHILDREN OF THE MOST HIGH:
PRISTINE YOUTH AND FAMILY SOLUTIONS, LLC.
SONS AND DAUGHTERS OF THE MOST HIGH PUBLISHERS ®

Oh, Gracious Most High Heavenly father, Holy is your name, Your Will Be Done Now and Forever!

References

Gibran, K. (1968). Secrets of the Heart. Hallmark Cards Inc.

Harris, D. Jacqueline (2010). Healing and Freedom Through These Sacred Tone Masters.

Houghton Mifflin Company. (2020). Online American Heritage Dictionary. Fifth Edition.

Leaf, C. M. Switch On Your Brain: The Key to Peak Happiness, Thinking, and Health. 2013.

Lyubomirsky, S., King, L., & Diener, E. (2005). The benefits of frequent positive affect: Does happiness lead to success? Psychological bulletin, 131(6), 803.

Mchie, Benjamin (2019). African American Registry® (the Registry).

209

"And whatsoever we ask, we receive of him, because we keep his commandments, and do those things that are pleasing in his sight, KJV 1 John 3:22."

Beware of the Pink Assassin (Your Tongue): The True Vine
(Yashu'a, Jesus) Power of Life and Death is in the Tongue;
**Speaking God's (אלהים Elóhîym) "Will"
for Your Life into Existence!**

CHILDREN OF THE MOST HIGH:
PRISTINE YOUTH AND FAMILY SOLUTIONS, LLC.
SONS AND DAUGHTERS OF THE MOST HIGH PUBLISHERS ®

*Oh, Gracious Most High Heavenly father, Holy is your name,
Your Will Be Done Now and Forever!*

References

Ma, X., Yue, Z. Q., Gong, Z. Q., Zhang, H., Duan, N. Y., Shi,
Y. T., ... & Li, Y. F. (2017). The effect of diaphragmatic
breathing on attention, negative affect and stress in healthy
adults. *Frontiers in psychology*, *8*, 874.

Morse, Philip McCord, Acoustical Society of America, &
American Institute of Physics. (1948). Vibration and sound
(Vol. 2, pp. 326-328). New York: McGraw-Hill.

Newberg, M. D., & Andrew, B. (2012). Communication in
Health and Wellness: How Words Can Change Your Brain.

Online King James Version Blue Letter Bible, (2020).

Online King James Version Blue Letter bible Greek Strong's
Concordance, (2020).

Online Mayo Clinic Website, (2020).

Online New American Standard Bible, (2020).

Online Thayer King James Version Bible Lexicon (2011).

210

**"And whatsoever we ask, we receive of him,
because we keep his commandments, and do those
things that are pleasing in his sight, KJV 1 John 3:22."**

www.ingramcontent.com/pod-product-compliance
Lightning Source LLC
Chambersburg PA
CBHW071527040426
42452CB00008B/916